THE CHRISTMAS
Collection

CONTENTS

CHAPTER 1 Christmas Party 6

CHAPTER 2 Christmas Eve 50

CHAPTER 3 Christmas Morning 104

CHAPTER 4 Christmas Dinner 128

CHAPTER 5 Christmas Puddings & Desserts 192

CHAPTER 6 Christmas Cakes 238

CHAPTER 7 Edible Gifts 270

CHAPTER 8 Boxing Day 308

GLOSSARY 340
CONVERSION CHART 345
INDEX 346

CHAPTER 1
Christmas
PARTY

ON THE FIRST DAY
of Christmas

SILVER SPRAYED TWIGS
or tree branches make a great modern Christmas tree.
YOU WILL NEED a handful of tree branches
from the garden, roadside or from a flower shop,
a can of silver spray paint from a craft store, newspaper,
SILVER AND GLASS DECORATIONS, scissors,
white or silver ribbon and a vase. **PLACE THE TWIGS** or branches
on a large sheet of newspaper in a well-ventilated room.
Spray paint the twigs until well covered then leave to dry for 1 hour.
TURN THE BRANCHES over and spray the underside so all surfaces are silver.
Leave to dry for a further 30 minutes.
This can be repeated if necessary to **ENSURE FULL COVERAGE**.
ARRANGE THE TWIGS in a vase (choose a neutral colour such as white or
clear glass) and turn the twigs until you have a 'tree' shape you are happy with.
CUT THE RIBBON of your choice into lengths
(you will need as many lengths of ribbons as there are **DECORATIONS**).
Loop a strip of ribbon through each bauble
and tie the ends together,
HANG THE BAUBLES all over the tree carefully sliding the
ribbons over different twigs.

PECORINO AND NIGELLA SEED
Biscuits

PREP + COOK TIME *1 HOUR (+ REFRIGERATION)* **MAKES** *70*

1½ cups (225g) plain (all-purpose) flour
1 teaspoon nigella seeds
150g (5 ounces) butter, chopped coarsely
1¼ cups (100g) coarsely grated pecorino romano cheese
1 egg yolk

1. Sift flour into large bowl, add seeds; rub in butter and cheese. Add egg yolk; mix to a firm dough. Wrap in plastic; refrigerate 1 hour.
2. Divide dough into two portions, roll each portion on floured surface to 5mm (¼-inch) thick. Cut out stars using a 5cm (2-inch) cutter; place shapes on greased oven trays. Refrigerate biscuits 30 minutes.
3. Preheat oven to 180°C/350°F.
4. Bake biscuits about 20 minutes; cool on trays.

The dough can be shaped into a log, wrapped tightly in plastic and frozen. Remove, defrost in refrigerator and slice into 1cm (½-inch) rounds, place on an oven tray and bake as above. Store biscuits in an airtight container for up to 1 week.

MULLED "WINE" *Cocktail*

PREP + COOK TIME 20 MINUTES (+ REFRIGERATION) SERVES 8

Combine 2 litres (8 cups) red grape juice, 4 strips orange rind, 2 tablespoons light brown sugar, 2 cinnamon sticks, 12 cloves, 3 fresh bay leaves and 2 sprigs fresh thyme in large saucepan. Simmer, uncovered, about 10 minutes (do not boil). Cool; refrigerate until cold. Strain mixture into large jug; discard solids. Add 1 thinly sliced small orange, extra fresh bay leaves and fresh sprigs of thyme. Serve over ice.

SPARKLING *Raspberry*

PREP TIME 25 MINUTES (+ REFRIGERATION) SERVES 8

Combine 180g (6 ounces) fresh or frozen raspberries, ⅓ cup strawberry-flavoured liqueur, ⅓ cup orange-flavoured liqueur, 1 tablespoon caster (superfine) sugar and the zest of ½ small orange in small bowl. Refrigerate 20 minutes, stirring occasionally, until sugar dissolves. Divide mixture into eight glasses; top with 3 cups chilled sparkling white wine.

Zest the orange into long thin strips.

LYCHEE AND LIME *Muddle*

PREP + COOK TIME 30 MINUTES (+ REFRIGERATION) SERVES 8

Thinly slice 12 fresh kaffir lime leaves and a 6cm (2¼-inch) piece fresh ginger; place in a small saucepan with 2 cups water and ¼ cup grated palm sugar. Stir over medium heat until sugar dissolves; bring to the boil. Reduce heat; simmer, uncovered, until reduced to 1½ cups. Strain syrup into medium heatproof jug; discard solids. Cool; refrigerate until cold. Divide 1kg (2 pounds) seeded lychees, 1 quartered and thinly sliced lime, 1⅓ cups white rum, ⅓ cup lime juice and the syrup into eight glasses; gently crush and mix with muddling stick (or the handle of a thick wooden spoon or a pestle). Top with ice and 2 cups chilled soda water.

A muddling stick is a bartender's tool used to crush or mash fruits, herbs and spices in the bottom of a glass to release their flavour.

APPLE *Pimm's*

PREP TIME 15 MINUTES SERVES 8

Combine 2 cups cucumber juice, 1⅓ cups Pimm's, 1.5 litres (6 cups) chilled sparkling apple juice, 1 cup ginger wine, 1 thinly sliced lebanese cucumber, 1 quartered and thinly sliced medium red apple and 1 cup loosely packed fresh mint leaves in large jug. Serve over ice.

Juice about 800g (1½ pounds) peeled cucumbers in a juicer separator. Or, puree peeled cucumber in blender or processor, strain into a jug and discard the solids. Pimm's is a gin-based alcohol flavoured with herbs.

Christmas Party

CAMPARI, ORANGE *and Soda*

PREP TIME 10 MINUTES **SERVES** 8

Combine 1 cup campari, 3 cups chilled orange or tropical juice and 2 cups chilled soda water in large jug. Thinly slice 1 small orange; halve slices. Divide orange slices and ½ cup fresh or frozen blueberries into eight serving glasses. Pour over campari mixture. Serve with ice.

When in season, use blood oranges.

CLASSIC COSMOPOLITAN *Cocktail*

PREP TIME 10 MINUTES (+ REFRIGERATION) **SERVES** 8

Combine 1¼ cups vodka, ⅓ cup orange-flavoured liqueur, ½ cup lime juice and 2½ cups chilled cranberry-pomegranate juice in large jug. Refrigerate 1 hour. Just before serving, stir in 2½ cups chilled lemonade, 1 thinly sliced lime and ½ cup loosely packed fresh mint leaves. Serve with ice.

WHITE CHOCOLATE *Eggnog*

PREP + COOK TIME 20 MINUTES **SERVES** 8

Bring 3 cups milk to the boil in medium saucepan. Remove from heat. Meanwhile, whisk 4 egg yolks and ⅓ cup caster (superfine) sugar in medium bowl until combined. Gradually whisk in hot milk. Return eggnog mixture to pan; stir over low heat, without boiling, until mixture is thick enough to coat the back of a spoon. Remove from heat. Add 90g (3 ounces) finely chopped white chocolate, 2 tablespoons brandy and 2 tablespoons rum; stir until smooth. Beat ¾ cup thickened (heavy) cream in small bowl with electric mixer until soft peaks form. Pour eggnog into eight warmed heatproof ¾ cup (180ml) serving glasses; top with cream. Serve sprinkled with nutmeg.

PINEAPPLE PASSIONFRUIT *Spritzer*

PREP TIME 5 MINUTES **SERVES** 8

Combine 340g (11 ounces) canned passionfruit pulp in syrup, 1 litre (4 cups) chilled pineapple juice, 3 cups (750ml) chilled sparkling mineral water and ½ cup coarsely chopped fresh mint in large jug. Serve with ice.

To make an alcoholic version, replace mineral water with sparkling white wine.

SALT, LEMON AND
Rosemary Cured Beef

PREP + COOK TIME 40 MINUTES (+ REFRIGERATION) MAKES 36

500g (1-pound) piece beef eye fillet
36 thin slices sourdough bread stick
¼ cup (60ml) olive oil
⅓ cup (80g) sour cream
⅓ cup (15g) mustard cress

LEMON AND ROSEMARY SALT CURE
1 cup (125g) salt flakes
1 cup (220g) raw sugar
⅓ cup loosely packed fresh rosemary sprigs, chopped coarsely
2 tablespoons finely chopped lemon rind
1 teaspoon black peppercorns
½ cup (125ml) vermouth or vodka

1. Make lemon and rosemary salt cure.
2. Place two sheets of plastic wrap, long enough to enclose beef, overlapping by half, on bench; spread with half the salt cure. Place beef on top, cover beef with remaining salt cure; wrap beef tightly in plastic, place on large deep tray. Top with smaller tray or board; weigh down with bricks or food cans. Refrigerate 12 hours. Remove weights, turn beef over; replace tray and weights, refrigerate a further 12 hours.
3. Preheat grill (broiler).
4. Place bread slices on oven trays; brush with oil, toast each side lightly.
5. Unwrap beef, wipe salt cure away; thinly slice beef. Spread sour cream over toast, top with beef, sprinkle with cress.

LEMON AND ROSEMARY SALT CURE
Using a mortar and pestle, pound ¼ cup of the salt, ¼ cup of the sugar, and the rosemary, rind and pepper to a fine powder. Transfer to medium bowl, stir in vermouth and remaining salt and sugar.

You need the freshest, best quality beef for this recipe. Use a vegetable peeler to remove strips of rind from the lemon before chopping. Beef will keep, in an airtight container, in the fridge for up to one week.

CHICKEN AND PORT PATE
on Polenta Crisps

PREP + COOK TIME 50 MINUTES (+ REFRIGERATION)   MAKES 48

50g (1½ ounces) butter, softened
300g (9½ ounces) chicken livers, trimmed
2 shallots (50g), chopped finely
1 clove garlic, crushed
2 tablespoons port
½ cup (100g) drained seeded sour cherries
48 fresh chervil sprigs

POLENTA CRISPS
1 cup (250ml) water
2 cups (500ml) chicken stock
¾ cup (125g) polenta
30g (1 ounce) butter
vegetable oil, for deep-frying

1. Make polenta crisps.
2. Meanwhile, heat half the butter in medium frying pan; cook livers, in batches, until just browned. Remove from pan.
3. Cook shallot and garlic in same pan, stirring, until shallot softens. Add port; cook, uncovered, until almost all of the liquid has evaporated.
4. Blend or process livers with shallot mixture until smooth. Push mixture through sieve; discard solids.
5. Blend or process pâté mixture with remaining butter until smooth. Transfer to small bowl, cover; refrigerate 2 hours.
6. Serve pâté on polenta crisps, topped with a cherry and a sprig of chervil.

POLENTA CRISPS
Oil 8cm x 25cm (3¼-inch x 10-inch) bar cake pan. Bring the water and stock to the boil in medium saucepan; gradually add polenta, stirring constantly. Reduce heat; simmer, stirring, about 10 minutes or until polenta thickens. Stir in butter then spread polenta into pan; cool 10 minutes. Cover; refrigerate about 2 hours or until firm. Turn polenta onto board, trim edges; cut in half lengthways, then slice into 1cm (½-inch) pieces. Heat oil in wok; deep-fry polenta, in batches, until browned. Drain on absorbent paper.

GREEN ONION BLINIS
with Chilli Crab Salad

PREP + COOK TIME *40 MINUTES (+ COOLING)* **MAKES 24**

⅔ cup (100g) wholemeal plain (all-purpose) flour
⅓ cup (50g) white self-raising flour
½ teaspoon cayenne pepper
2 eggs
¾ cup (180ml) buttermilk
2 green onions (scallions), sliced finely
40g (1½ ounces) butter, melted

CHILLI CRAB SALAD
150g (4½ ounces) cooked crab meat
1 tablespoon each finely chopped fresh mint and vietnamese mint
1 teaspoon finely grated lime rind
2 tablespoons lime juice
2 teaspoons fish sauce
½ lebanese cucumber (65g), seeded, chopped finely
1 fresh small red thai (serrano) chilli, sliced thinly

1 Sift flours and pepper into medium bowl; whisk in eggs and buttermilk until smooth. Stir in onion and butter.
2 Heat oiled large frying pan; cook level tablespoons of blini mixture, in batches, until golden both sides. Cool on wire racks.
3 Meanwhile, make chilli crab salad.
4 Serve blinis topped with salad.

CHILLI CRAB SALAD
Combine ingredients in medium bowl; season to taste.

You could serve the crab mixture on mini toasts, lavash or sliced french bread stick. You can buy cooked crab meat at the local fish markets or supermarket. Alternatively, buy fresh crabs and cook them (blue swimmer crabs are good). To tell if crabs are meaty, look at the claws; if they are pointy and sharp it means they have a new shell and don't have much meat. If the claws are rounded, they have an older shell and will have more meat.

CROSTINI WITH FETTA,
Artichokes and Rocket

CROSTINI WITH FETTA,
Artichokes and Rocket

PREP + COOK TIME 20 MINUTES SERVES 6

1 small french bread stick (150g), sliced thinly
olive-oil spray
1 clove garlic, halved
30g (1 ounce) baby rocket (arugula) leaves
1 teaspoon extra virgin olive oil
1 teaspoon red wine vinegar
5 drained marinated artichoke hearts (60g),
  cut into 6 wedges each
100g (3 ounces) fetta cheese, crumbled

1 Preheat oven to 180°C/350°F.
2 To make crostini, spray both sides of bread slices with olive-oil spray; toast on oven tray until browned both sides and crisp. Rub one side of each crostini with cut-side of garlic; place crostini on platter.
3 Combine rocket with oil and vinegar in medium bowl; season to taste.
4 Top crostini with rocket mixture, artichokes and cheese then freshly cracked black pepper.

If you don't have the time to make the crostini, ready-made crostini can be found in various flavours in most delicatessens and some supermarkets.

SCALLOPS
with Saffron Cream

PREP + COOK TIME 15 MINUTES (+ STANDING) MAKES 12

12 scallops in half shell (480g)
1 teaspoon olive oil
1 small brown onion (80g), chopped finely
2 teaspoons finely grated lemon rind
pinch saffron threads
⅔ cup (160ml) pouring cream
1 tablespoon lemon juice
2 teaspoons salmon roe

1 Remove scallops from shells; wash and dry shells. Place shells, in single layer, on serving platter.
2 Rinse scallops under cold water; discard scallop roe. Gently pat scallops dry with absorbent paper.
3 Heat oil in small saucepan; cook onion, stirring, until softened. Add rind, saffron and cream; bring to the boil. Reduce heat; simmer, uncovered, about 5 minutes or until mixture has reduced to about ½ cup. Remove from heat; stand 30 minutes. Stir in juice; stand 10 minutes. Strain cream mixture into small bowl then back into same cleaned pan; stir over low heat until heated through.
4 Meanwhile, cook scallops, in batches, on heated oiled grill plate (or grill or barbecue) until browned lightly and cooked as desired.
5 Return scallops to shells; top with cream sauce and salmon roe.

(PHOTOGRAPH PAGE 24)

Christmas Party

SCALLOPS
with Saffron Cream
(RECIPE PAGE 23)

WARM ORANGE
and Fennel Olives
(RECIPE PAGE 26)

WARM ORANGE and Fennel Olives

PREP + COOK TIME 10 MINUTES SERVES 6

1 medium orange (240g)
400g (12½ ounces) mixed marinated seeded olives
½ cup (125ml) dry red wine
1 teaspoon coarsely cracked black pepper
½ teaspoon fennel seeds

1 Using a vegetable peeler, peel thin strips of rind from orange.
2 Place rind, olives, wine, pepper and fennel seeds in medium saucepan; bring to a simmer. Remove from heat; stand 10 minutes before serving warm.

SERVING SUGGESTION
Serve warm olives with grissini breadsticks and cheese.

(PHOTOGRAPH PAGE 25)

QUAIL EGGS with Dukkah

PREP + COOK TIME 15 MINUTES MAKES 24

24 quail eggs
¼ cup (30g) dukkah
¼ cup loosely packed fresh chervil sprigs

1 Place eggs in a single layer in wide saucepan. Barely cover eggs with water; cover, bring to the boil. Boil for 1½ minutes; drain eggs, rinse with cold water. Crack shell of each egg; place eggs in bowl of cold water. Shell eggs under cold water.
2 Sprinkle eggs with dukkah; serve on a bed of sea salt flakes sprinkled with chervil.

QUAIL EGGS
with Dukkah

HOT SMOKED TROUT
with Young Coconut

PREP + COOK TIME 40 MINUTES MAKES 24

1 medium pomelo (680g), segmented
200g (6½ ounces) flaked hot-smoked trout
100g (3 ounces) coconut flesh, sliced thinly
1 cup loosely packed small thai basil leaves
1 cup loosely packed small fresh coriander (cilantro) leaves
24 betel leaves
¼ cup (35g) crushed roasted peanuts
¼ cup (50g) salmon roe

PEANUT NAM JIM
¼ cup (35g) roasted unsalted peanuts
¼ cup (65g) grated palm sugar
¼ cup (60ml) fish sauce
1 fresh small green thai (serrano) chilli, chopped finely
1cm (½-inch) piece fresh ginger (5g), grated finely
1 teaspoon finely grated lime rind
¼ cup (60ml) lime juice
1 tablespoon reserved coconut liquid

1. Make peanut nam jim.
2. Break pomelo segments into small pieces; place in large bowl. Add trout, coconut and three-quarters of the combined herbs.
3. Place betel leaves on serving platter; top with trout mixture. Drizzle with peanut nam jim, sprinkle with remaining herbs, peanuts and salmon roe.

PEANUT NAM JIM
Lightly grease an oven tray; sprinkle with peanuts. Heat sugar and 2 teaspoons of the fish sauce in small saucepan; cook about 2 minutes or until lightly caramelised. Pour over peanuts; cool until set then break into pieces. Using mortar and pestle (or blender or food processor) pound pieces into a fine powder. Place in small bowl; stir in remaining ingredients.

Fresh coconuts are available in the fresh produce section of most supermarkets. To open a fresh coconut, pierce one of the eyes; drain the liquid and reserve for the peanut nam jim. Roast coconut briefly in a very hot oven until cracks appear in the shell. Cool, then break the coconut apart. Use a metal spoon to remove the flesh.

Christmas Party

SPICED EGGPLANT
and Haloumi Tarts

PREP + COOK TIME *50 MINUTES* **MAKES** *30*

1 medium eggplant (300g), peeled, chopped coarsely
1 teaspoon each ground coriander and cumin
2 tablespoons olive oil
¼ cup (55g) firmly packed light brown sugar
¼ cup (60ml) water
¼ cup (60ml) lime juice (see tip)
2 tablespoons finely chopped fresh flat-leaf parsley
100g (3 ounces) haloumi cheese, sliced thickly
2 tablespoons lemon juice
1 teaspoon finely cracked black pepper
30 baked mini shortcrust or puff pastry tart shells

1 Preheat oven to 200°C/400°F.
2 Toss eggplant, cumin, coriander and oil in small baking dish; season. Cover dish; roast 20 minutes. Remove cover; roast 10 minutes or until eggplant is tender.
3 Combine sugar and the water in small saucepan; stir over heat until sugar dissolves.
4 Blend or process eggplant mixture, sugar syrup and lime juice until eggplant is coarsely chopped. Stir in parsley; cover to keep warm.
5 Sprinkle cheese with lemon juice and pepper; cook on heated barbecue (or grill or grill plate) until browned both sides. Cut cheese into 30 pieces.
6 Fill tart shells with warm eggplant mixture; top with cheese, and fine shreds of lime rind.

Shred thin strips of rind from lime, to garnish tarts, before juicing. Mini shortcrust and puff pastry tart shells are available from most major supermarkets and delicatessens. For an earthier flavour, barbecue the whole eggplant. Prick the skin all over with a fork, then cook the eggplant for about 30 minutes (depending on its size and the heat of the barbecue) or until the eggplant collapses. Cool the eggplant, peel away the skin, then proceed with the recipe.

WASABI AND SAKE
Cured Kingfish

PREP + COOK TIME *1 HOUR (+ REFRIGERATION)* **SERVES 12**

1kg (2 pounds) sashimi-quality white fish fillets
2 teaspoons black sesame seeds
WASABI AND SAKE CURE
1⅔ cups (500g) rock salt
1¾ cups (385g) white (granulated) sugar
¼ cup (60ml) sake
2 tablespoons wasabi powder
1 cup (10g) shredded nori
PICKLED DAIKON
200g (6½ ounces) daikon
½ cup (5g) shredded nori
½ cup (125ml) mirin
1 tablespoon rice wine vinegar
1 teaspoon salt

1 Make wasabi and sake cure.
2 Place two sheets of plastic wrap, long enough to enclose fish, overlapping by half, on bench; spread with half the cure mixture. Place fish on top, cover with remaining cure; wrap tightly in plastic, place on large deep tray. Top with smaller tray or board, weigh down with food cans; refrigerate 12 hours. Remove weights, turn fish over; replace tray and weights, refrigerate a further 12 hours.
3 Meanwhile, make pickled daikon.
4 Unwrap fish, wipe off cure. Using a sharp knife, thinly slice fish. Place fish on platter, sprinkle with seeds; serve with pickled daikon.

WASABI AND SAKE CURE
Combine ingredients in medium bowl.

PICKLED DAIKON
Using a vegetable peeler, peel daikon into ribbons. Place in medium bowl with nori. Stir mirin, vinegar and salt in small saucepan over high heat, until salt is dissolved; simmer, uncovered, 5 minutes. Pour over daikon; cool.

Any type of sashimi-quality white fish can be used for this recipe; we used kingfish.

O CHRISTMAS TREE
O Christmas tree

NOT EVERYONE HAS room for a large tree so why not buy a small tree and use it as a **TABLE SETTING**. **YOU WILL NEED** a small Christmas tree (available from specialist suppliers), a garden urn or ornate bucket and a small bag of pebbles (available from garden centres), as well as **SCISSORS AND BAUBLES**. **PLACE THE STEM** of the tree in the urn or bucket and fill the space around with pebbles **OR SMALL STONES** to keep the tree in an upright position. Using scissors, trim the tips from any branches that stick out irregularly to give the tree that **CLASSIC TREE SHAPE**. **HANG A SELECTION** of small baubles at intervals on the tree. Choose a **SIMPLE COLOUR PALETTE** of two contrasting colours as with the *gold and green* seen here.

SALMON Ceviche

PREP + COOK TIME 30 MINUTES SERVES 10

500g (1-pound) salmon fillet, skinned, chopped finely
¼ cup (60ml) lime juice
¼ cup (60ml) extra virgin olive oil
2 lebanese cucumbers (340g), chopped finely
1 small avocado (200g), chopped finely
1 shallot (25g), chopped finely
½ cup coarsely chopped fresh coriander (cilantro)
10 long slices bread, (see note)
1 clove garlic, halved

1. Combine salmon, juice, 2 tablespoons of the oil, cucumber, avocado, shallot and coriander in large bowl; season to taste. Spoon into 10 small glasses; cover, refrigerate 15 minutes.
2. Meanwhile, preheat grill (broiler). Brush bread with remaining oil; toast both sides under grill. Rub toast with cut-sides of garlic.
3. Serve ceviche with garlic toast.

We used a baguette for the garlic toast.
If making this dish a few hours ahead, combine ingredients, except for cucumber, in large bowl; toss cucumber through just before serving. The longer the salmon marinates with the lime, the more 'cooked' it will be.

BLINIS with Goat's Cheese

PREP + COOK TIME 40 MINUTES MAKES 48

¼ cup (35g) buckwheat flour
½ cup (100g) plain (all-purpose) flour
1½ teaspoons baking powder
¾ cup (180ml) milk
1 egg
50g (1½ ounces) butter, melted
⅓ cup (80g) soft goat's cheese
2 tablespoons light sour cream
1½ tablespoons cranberry sauce
⅔ cup small fresh mint leaves

1. Sift flours and baking powder into large bowl. Whisk in milk, egg and half the butter until smooth.
2. Whisk cheese and cream together in small bowl; season to taste.
3. Heat large frying pan on medium heat; grease with a little remaining butter. Cook heaped teaspoons of batter, in batches, about 1 minute each side or until golden.
4. Top each warm blini with cheese mixture, sauce and mint.

You can make the blinis a few hours ahead; reheat, covered with foil, in a 100°C/210°F oven about 5 minutes. Assemble just before serving. Remove goat's cheese from refrigerator 30 minutes before using to soften it.

Christmas Party

SALMON *Ceviche*

BLINIS *with Goat's Cheese*

SMOKED CHICKEN
Crostini

SMOKED CHICKEN
Crostini

PREP + COOK TIME 30 MINUTES MAKES 24

1½ cups (180g) shredded smoked chicken
2 shallots (50g), chopped finely
¼ cup (30g) finely chopped celery
¼ cup (25g) walnuts, roasted, chopped coarsely
1 tablespoon finely chopped fresh tarragon
¼ cup (75g) mayonnaise
1 teaspoon wholegrain mustard
1 tablespoon preserved lemon rind, chopped finely
1 small french bread stick (150g), cut into 24 slices
1 large clove garlic, halved
2 tablespoons olive oil
1 small pear (180g), cut into matchsticks

1. Combine chicken, shallot, celery, nuts, tarragon, mayonnaise, mustard and preserved lemon in medium bowl.
2. Toast bread slices, in batches, on heated grill plate (or grill or barbecue). Rub one side with cut-side of garlic, brush with oil; season to taste.
3. Serve crostini topped with chicken mixture and pear.

Chicken mixture can be prepared a day ahead; keep, covered, in the refrigerator. Preserved lemons can be bought from delis and some supermarkets. Remove a piece of lemon from the jar, discard the lemon flesh. Rinse the rind under water, dry, then chop finely.

ZUCCHINI AND CORN FRITTERS
with Crème Fraîche

PREP + COOK TIME 40 MINUTES (+ STANDING) MAKES 50

½ cup (75g) plain (all-purpose) flour
½ cup (75g) self-raising flour
2 eggs
½ cup (140g) yogurt
½ teaspoon caster (superfine) sugar
410g (13 ounces) canned corn kernels, drained
2 small zucchini (180g), grated coarsely
2 cloves garlic, crushed
1 small red onion (100g), chopped finely
2 tablespoons finely chopped fresh basil
1 tablespoon finely chopped fresh tarragon
¼ cup (20g) finely grated parmesan cheese
2 tablespoons olive oil
¾ cup (180g) crème fraîche
⅓ cup (50g) pine nuts, roasted
⅓ cup small fresh basil leaves

1. Sift flours into large bowl; whisk in eggs, yogurt and sugar. Stir in corn, zucchini, garlic, onion, chopped herbs and cheese; stand 15 minutes.
2. Heat oil in large frying pan; cook heaped teaspoons of fritter mixture, in batches, until browned both sides. Cool on wire racks.
3. Serve fritters topped with crème fraîche, pine nuts and basil leaves.

Fresh corn can be used instead of canned corn; you will need two cobs. Sour cream or yogurt can be used instead of the crème fraîche. Fritters can be made the day before; top them with crème fraîche etc, an hour or so before serving.

(PHOTOGRAPH PAGE 40)

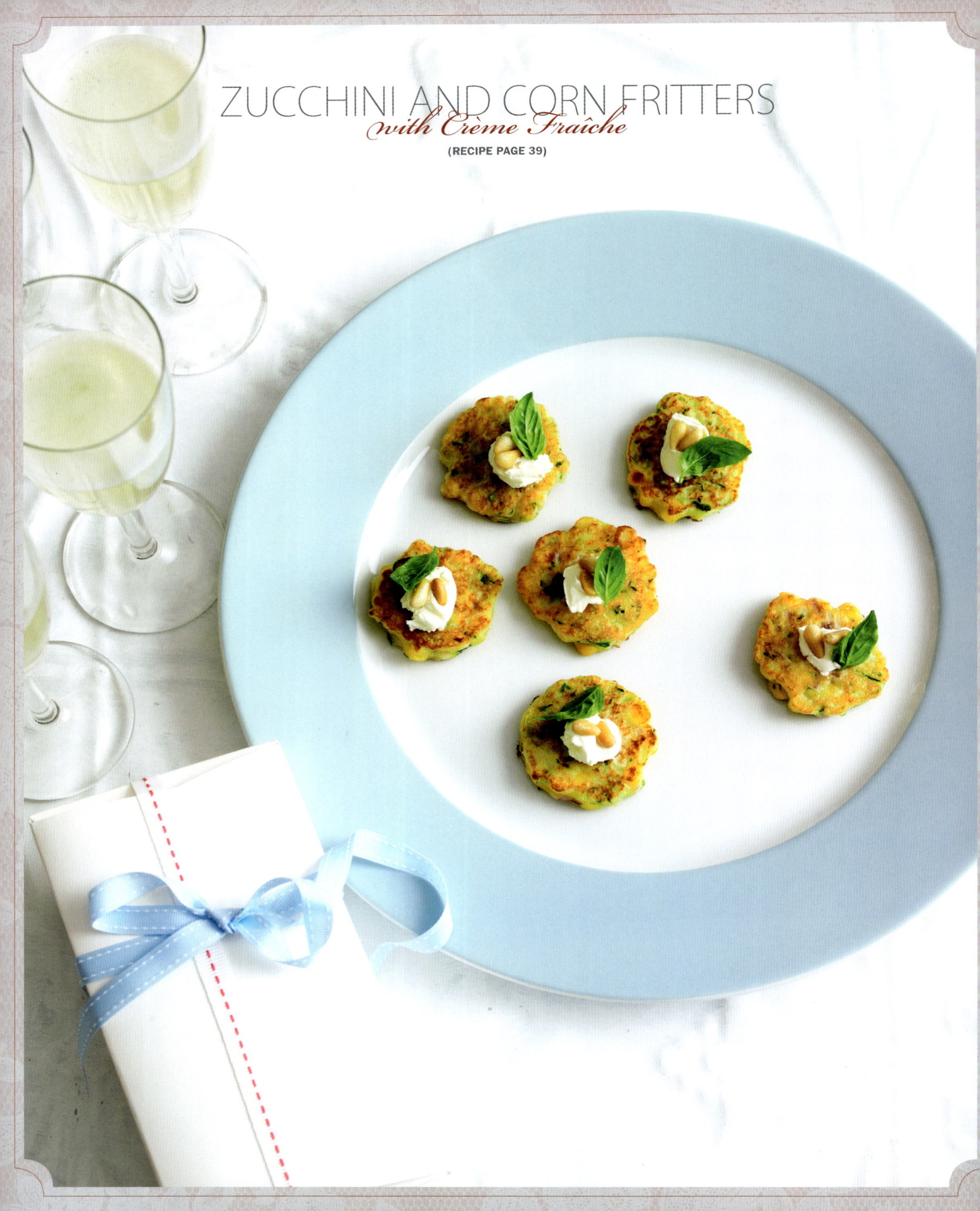

ZUCCHINI AND CORN FRITTERS
with Crème Fraîche
(RECIPE PAGE 39)

SWEET POTATO, MINT
and Goat's Cheese Tartlets
(RECIPE PAGE 42)

SWEET POTATO, MINT and Goat's Cheese Tartlets

PREP + COOK TIME 35 MINUTES MAKES 24

4 sheets fillo pastry
50g (1½ ounces) butter, melted
1 small kumara (orange sweet potato) (300g), chopped coarsely
¼ cup finely chopped fresh mint
100g (3 ounces) soft goat's cheese, crumbled
24 small fresh mint leaves

1. Preheat oven to 200°C/400°F. Grease two 12-hole (1-tablespoon/20ml) mini muffin pans.
2. Layer pastry sheets, brushing each with butter. Cut pastry stack into 24 x 7cm (2¾-inch) squares; line pan holes with squares. Bake about 5 minutes or until browned lightly; cool in pans.
3. Meanwhile, boil, steam or microwave kumara until tender; drain. Cool. Mash kumara in medium bowl with chopped mint until smooth; season to taste.
4. Divide mash between tartlet shells. Top with cheese and mint.

Tartlet shells will keep in an airtight container for up to one week.

(PHOTOGRAPH PAGE 41)

SKEWERED PRAWNS with Chilli Marinade

PREP + COOK TIME 30 MINUTES (+ REFRIGERATION) MAKES 24

24 uncooked medium king prawns (shrimp) (1kg)
3 limes
1 tablespoon peanut oil
2 fresh kaffir lime leaves, shredded finely
5mm (¼-inch) piece fresh ginger (2.5g), grated
2 teaspoons sambal oelek
1 teaspoon sesame oil
2 tablespoons japanese soy sauce
2 tablespoons mirin

1. Shell and devein prawns leaving tails intact. Quarter limes lengthways; cut each quarter in half lengthways to give a total of 24 wedges. Thread prawns onto skewers; followed by a lime wedge.
2. Combine remaining ingredients in small bowl; season to taste. Brush skewers with half the marinade. Cover, refrigerate 1 hour.
3. Cook skewers, in batches, on heated oiled grill plate (or grill or barbecue) until prawns are changed in colour, brushing with remaining marinade occasionally. Serve immediately.

You need 24 bamboo skewers for this recipe; soak them in cold water for at least an hour before using to prevent scorching during cooking.

MUSTARD BEEF
Canapés

PREP + COOK TIME 15 MINUTES MAKES 24

2 tablespoons wholegrain mustard
2 tablespoons horseradish cream
2 beef new york-cut steaks (440g)
2 teaspoons olive oil
¼ cup (60g) sour cream
24 baby spinach leaves
CROSTINI
1 small french bread stick (150g)
cooking-oil spray

1. Combine half the mustard and half the horseradish in small bowl; spread over steaks. Cover; refrigerate.
2. Meanwhile, make crostini.
3. Heat oil in large frying pan; cook steaks, uncovered, until cooked as desired. Cover; stand 5 minutes then slice thinly.
4. Combine remaining mustard and horseradish with sour cream in small bowl. Top crostini with spinach, steak slices and sour cream mixture.

CROSTINI
Preheat oven to 160°C/325°F. Discard ends of bread; cut bread into 1cm (½-inch) slices. Place slices, in single layer, on oven tray; spray with oil. Toast, both sides, in oven until browned lightly and crisp.

New york-cut steaks are also known as sirloin or striploin, without the bone.

LAMB CUTLETS
with Sumac Yogurt

PREP + COOK TIME 30 MINUTES (+ REFRIGERATION) MAKES 24

2 tablespoons za'atar
¼ cup (60ml) olive oil
1 tablespoon dried oregano
2 cloves garlic, crushed
2 teaspoons finely grated lemon rind
2 tablespoons lemon juice
24 french-trimmed lamb cutlets (1.2kg)
48 small fresh mint leaves
SUMAC YOGURT
1 cup (280g) yogurt
1 clove garlic, crushed
1 lebanese cucumber (130g), seeded, chopped finely
2 teaspoons sumac

1. Combine za'atar, oil, oregano, garlic, rind and juice in large bowl; add lamb, turn to coat in mixture. Cover; refrigerate 3 hours or overnight.
2. Make sumac yogurt.
3. Cook cutlets, in batches, on heated oiled barbecue (or grill or grill plate).
4. Serve cutlets warm, topped with sumac yogurt and two mint leaves each.

SUMAC YOGURT
Combine ingredients in small bowl; season to taste.

Lamb can be marinated and sumac yogurt made a day ahead; keep, covered, in the refrigerator. Za'atar is a Middle-Eastern herb and spice mix made with sumac, thyme, roasted sesame seeds, marjoram, oregano and sea salt; it is available from spice shops, Middle-Eastern food shops and delicatessens. A moroccan spice blend, available from supermarkets, can be used instead.

(PHOTOGRAPH PAGE 46)

LAMB CUTLETS
with Sumac Yogurt
(RECIPE PAGE 45)

CHICKEN CAESAR
on Baby Cos Leaves
(RECIPE PAGE 48)

CHICKEN CAESAR
on Baby Cos Leaves

PREP + COOK TIME 30 MINUTES MAKES 24

2 slices (90g) day-old white bread, crusts removed
2 slices prosciutto (30g)
1 cup (160g) shredded barbecued chicken
⅓ cup (80ml) caesar dressing
½ cup (40g) flaked parmesan cheese
2 baby cos (romaine) lettuce (360g)

1 Preheat grill (broiler).
2 Cut bread into 1cm (½-inch) squares, place on oven tray; grill until croûtons are browned lightly all over.
3 Place prosciutto on oven tray; grill until crisp. Drain on absorbent paper; chop coarsely.
4 Combine croûtons and prosciutto in medium bowl with chicken, dressing and ⅓ cup of the cheese; toss gently, season to taste.
5 Trim end from each lettuce; separate leaves (you need 24 small leaves). Place one level tablespoon of the caesar mixture on each leaf; sprinkle with remaining cheese.

You need about a quarter of a large barbecued chicken to get the amount of shredded meat required for this recipe.

(PHOTOGRAPH PAGE 47)

OYSTERS WITH CHILLI
and Ginger Dressing

PREP + COOK TIME 20 MINUTES MAKES 24

2 green onions (scallions), sliced thinly
24 oysters (600g) on the half shell
CHILLI AND GINGER DRESSING
1 dried red thai (serrano) chilli
½ cup (125ml) rice wine vinegar
2½ tablespoons white (granulated) sugar
2 teaspoons sea salt
2cm (¾-inch) piece fresh ginger (10g), cut into thin strips

1 Fill a small bowl with iced water; add onion. Stand until onion curls.
2 Meanwhile, make chilli and ginger dressing.
3 Place oysters on serving platter. Drizzle with dressing; top with a little reserved ginger and onion. Or, serve chilli and ginger dressing separately as a dipping sauce.

CHILLI AND GINGER DRESSING
Dry-fry chilli in small frying pan until blackened and puffed; cool. Using mortar and pestle, pound chilli to a fine powder. Combine ground chilli, vinegar, sugar, salt and half the ginger in small saucepan. Stir over low heat, without boiling, until sugar is dissolved. Bring to the boil; simmer, uncovered, without stirring, 5 minutes; cool.

Christmas Party

OYSTERS WITH CHILLI
and Ginger Dressing

CHAPTER 2
Christmas
EVE

CHRISTMAS
Wrappings

SPRUCE UP CHRISTMAS PRESENTS WITH A SPLASH OF CHRISTMAS FOLIAGE. Using foliage as a pretty decoration on your presents adds a personal touch that your friends and family will really appreciate. **YOU WILL NEED** your gifts, wrapping paper, scissors, sticky tape, secateurs, a basket or bag, and green ribbon. **WRAP ALL YOUR PRESENTS WITH THE SAME OR SIMILAR WRAPPING PAPER.** Using secateurs snip a few leaves from garden bushes or roadside trees. **PICK THOSE WITH VIBRANT GREEN FOLIAGE** and keep an eye out for any with red berries or flowers for a truly festive feel. **TRIM EACH SPRIG** to fit within the size of the present, place in the centre of the present and tie in place *with ribbon.*

CHICKEN, PORK AND VEAL *Terrine*

PREP + COOK TIME 1 HOUR 30 MINUTES (+ COOLING, REFRIGERATION & STANDING) SERVES 12

1 tablespoon olive oil
1 small brown onion (80g), chopped finely
2 cloves garlic, crushed
1 tablespoon finely chopped fresh thyme
1kg (2 pounds) minced (ground) pork and veal
¼ cup (60ml) brandy
2 tablespoons finely chopped fresh flat-leaf parsley
1 teaspoon ground allspice
½ teaspoon ground white pepper
⅓ cup (55g) pistachios, chopped coarsely
1 egg
1 teaspoon sea salt flakes
12 slices pancetta (180g)
4 chicken tenderloins (300g)

1. Preheat oven to 180°C/350°F. Heat oil in small frying pan; cook onion, garlic and thyme, stirring, until onion is soft. Transfer to large bowl; cool.
2. Add mince, brandy, parsley, allspice, pepper, nuts, egg and salt to onion mixture; mix well.
3. Grease 1.5-litre (6-cup) loaf pan (base measures 9cm x 25.5cm (3½ inches x 10 inches). Line base and long sides of pan with pancetta, extending pancetta over sides. Press one-third of the pork mixture into pan; top with two chicken tenderloins. Repeat layers with pork mixture and chicken, ending with pork layer. Fold over pancetta to enclose. Cover terrine with baking paper then foil.
4. Place pan in medium baking dish; pour enough boiling water into dish to come halfway up sides of pan. Bake about 50 minutes or until a metal skewer inserted into centre of terrine is warm to touch. Cool 15 minutes; refrigerate 3 hours or overnight.
5. Turn terrine onto board, remove jelly and fat. Transfer terrine to serving plate, stand 30 minutes before slicing.

SERVING SUGGESTION
Serve with cornichons, mustard, marinated figs and crusty bread.

Some butchers sell a pork and veal mixture; if it is not available as a mixture, buy 500g (1 pound) each of pork and veal mince.

Christmas Eve

FENNEL, RED ONION, GRAPEFRUIT
and Rocket Salad

PREP TIME *25 MINUTES* **SERVES** *8*

500g (1 pound) rocket (arugula)
1 small fennel bulb (200g), sliced thinly, fronds reserved
1 medium red onion (170g), sliced thinly
2 medium ruby red grapefruit (700g), segmented
1 lebanese cucumber (130g), cut into ribbons
⅓ cup loosely packed small fresh mint leaves

RED WINE VINEGAR MAYONNAISE
1 clove garlic, crushed
1 tablespoon red wine vinegar
2 tablespoons mayonnaise

1. Make red wine vinegar mayonnaise.
2. Combine rocket, fennel, onion, grapefruit, cucumber and mint on serving platter; drizzle with mayonnaise.
3. Serve salad sprinkled with fennel fronds.

RED WINE VINEGAR MAYONNAISE
Whisk ingredients in small jug until combined; season to taste.

If ruby red grapefruit are unavailable, use orange segments.

FIG, ONION AND *Bocconcini Tart*

PREP + COOK TIME *45 MINUTES* **SERVES** *8*

2 tablespoons olive oil
2 large red onions (600g), sliced finely
1 tablespoon finely chopped fresh thyme
1 tablespoon finely grated lemon rind
2 tablespoons light brown sugar
¼ cup (60ml) dry red wine
2 sheets puff pastry
1 egg, beaten lightly
10 fresh medium figs (600g), quartered
260g (8½ ounces) bocconcini cheese, drained, quartered
20g (¾ ounce) baby rocket (arugula) leaves

1. Preheat oven to 220°C/425°F.
2. Heat oil in large frying pan, add onion, thyme, rind and sugar; stir over medium heat, about 3 minutes or until onion is soft. Add wine; stir over low heat until wine has evaporated.
3. Line two oven trays with baking paper; place one pastry sheet on each. With the back of a knife, mark a 2cm (¾-inch) border around edge of each pastry sheet; brush border with egg, refrigerate 10 minutes.
4. Spread onion mixture over pastry sheets within borders; bake 10 minutes. Remove from oven, top with figs; bake about 10 minutes or until figs are browned.
5. Cut each tart into four; top with cheese and rocket, season to taste.

Use figs that are not too ripe. Overripe figs contain more moisture and will make the pastry soggy.

This simple elegant dish is an ideal starter. It's fresh, light, quick to make and visually impressive – all key elements when entertaining. With a variety of flavours and textures from crisp witlof and fennel to creamy smoked salmon, this platter sets the mood for the rest of the meal.

SMOKED SALMON
with Capers

PREP TIME *25 MINUTES* **SERVES** *8*

320g (10 ounces) sliced smoked salmon
1 small red onion (100g), chopped finely
½ cup (90g) drained, rinsed baby capers
2 small witlof (belgian endive) (110g), leaves separated
1 baby fennel bulb (130g), sliced thinly
2 red radishes (70g), trimmed, sliced thinly

MUSTARD HONEY DRESSING
1 teaspoon dijon mustard
2 teaspoons honey
2 tablespoons lemon juice
1 tablespoon finely chopped fresh dill
¼ cup (60ml) olive oil

1 Make mustard honey dressing.
2 Divide salmon between serving plates; sprinkle with onion and capers.
3 Serve salmon with witlof, fennel and radish; drizzle with dressing.

MUSTARD HONEY DRESSING
Place ingredients in screw-top jar; shake well. Season to taste.

ROAST TURKEY
with Prosciutto and Pear Stuffing

PREP + COOK TIME 3 HOURS 45 MINUTES (+ STANDING)   SERVES 12

5kg (10-pound) whole turkey
cooking-oil spray
¼ cup (35g) plain (all-purpose) flour
2 cups (500ml) chicken stock

PROSCIUTTO AND PEAR STUFFING
60g (2 ounces) butter
1 small leek (200g), sliced thinly
2 cloves garlic, crushed
8 slices prosciutto (120g), chopped finely
2 cups (140g) stale breadcrumbs
1 small pear (180g), chopped finely

HERB BUTTER
125g (4 ounces) butter, softened
2 cloves garlic, crushed
2 tablespoons finely chopped fresh sage
1 tablespoon each finely chopped fresh thyme and rosemary

1. Make prosciutto and pear stuffing.
2. Make herb butter.
3. Preheat oven to 180°C/350°F. Discard neck and giblets from turkey. Rinse turkey under cold water, pat dry inside and out with absorbent paper. Tuck wings under body. Loosen skin over breast and tops of legs using fingers or the handle of a wooden spoon. Push herb butter under skin of turkey, being careful not to break skin.
4. Fill turkey cavity with stuffing. Tie legs together with kitchen string. Place a wire rack in large baking dish. Place turkey on rack, tucking neck flap under body. Spray with oil; cover with foil. Roast for 2 hours; remove foil. Roast 40 minutes, basting occasionally with pan juices, or until juices run clear when the thickest part of the thigh is pierced with a skewer.
5. Transfer turkey to serving platter; cover loosely with foil. Stand 15 minutes.
6. Meanwhile, make gravy by skimming fat from pan drippings, leaving 2 tablespoons of drippings in dish. Place dish over high heat. Add flour; cook, stirring, until mixture thickens and bubbles. Gradually stir in stock; stir until mixture boils and thickens. Strain into serving jug.
7. Serve sliced turkey with gravy.

PROSCIUTTO AND PEAR STUFFING
Heat butter in medium frying pan; cook leek, garlic and prosciutto, stirring, until leek is tender. Stir in breadcrumbs; cook, stirring, 2 minutes or until toasted lightly. Remove from heat, stir in pear; season, cool.

HERB BUTTER
Combine ingredients in small bowl.

ROAST PORK
with Cranberry Sauce

PREP + COOK TIME *2 HOURS (+ STANDING)* **SERVES 8**

2kg (4-pound) boneless pork loin, rind on
60g (2 ounces) butter
1 tablespoon olive oil
1 medium red onion (170g), chopped finely
1 clove garlic, crushed
100g (3 ounces) mild salami, chopped finely
¼ cup (35g) roasted unsalted pistachios
¼ cup (35g) dried cranberries
1 tablespoon finely chopped fresh sage
½ cup (35g) stale breadcrumbs
2 tablespoons fine table salt
1½ cups (375ml) chicken stock
½ cup (125ml) port
¼ cup (80g) cranberry sauce

ROASTED VEGETABLES
500g (1 pound) pumpkin, cut into wedges
2 medium parsnips (500g), quartered
2 medium red onions (340g), quartered
500g (1 pound) baby carrots, trimmed
12 baby new potatoes (480g), halved
¼ cup (60ml) olive oil
2 tablespoons fresh thyme leaves

1. Preheat oven to 200°C/400°F.
2. Using sharp knife, score pork skin by making shallow cuts at 1cm (½-inch) intervals. Place pork on board, fat-side down; slice through thickest part of pork horizontally, without cutting through other side. Open pork out to form one large piece. Trim pork; reserve 150g (5 ounces) trimmings for seasoning. Blend or process pork trimmings with 20g (¾ ounce) of the butter; transfer to large bowl.
3. Heat oil in medium frying pan; cook onion and garlic, stirring, until onion softens. Add remaining butter, salami, nuts, cranberries and sage; cook 2 minutes. Transfer mixture to medium bowl; cool. Stir in breadcrumbs and minced trimmings.
4. Press seasoning mixture along one long side of pork; roll pork to enclose filling, secure with kitchen string at 2cm (¾-inch) intervals. Rub pork skin with salt; place on wire rack in large flameproof baking dish. Roast pork, uncovered, about 1¼ hours or until pork is cooked through.
5. Meanwhile, make roasted vegetables.
6. Remove pork from dish, cover loosely with foil; stand 15 minutes. Drain excess fat from dish, add stock, port and sauce to dish; stir over heat until sauce is reduced by half. Season to taste; cover to keep warm.
7. Serve sliced pork with sauce and vegetables.

ROASTED VEGETABLES
Combine vegetables in large baking dish with oil and thyme. Roast, uncovered, for last 30 minutes of pork cooking time, turning once. Season to taste.

Ask your butcher to leave a flap measuring about 20cm (8 inches) in length to help make rolling the loin easier.
The secret to exceptional crackling is to ensure the pork skin is dry and well-seasoned with fine salt before cooking. Pat the pork dry with absorbent paper; refrigerate, uncovered, for a few hours or overnight for the skin to dry out.

TRADITIONAL TURKEY
with Forcemeat Stuffing

PREP + COOK TIME 3 HOURS 50 MINUTES (+ STANDING) SERVES 10

4.5kg (9-pound) turkey
1 cup (250ml) water
80g (2½ ounces) butter, melted
¼ cup (35g) plain (all-purpose) flour
3 cups (750ml) chicken stock
½ cup (125ml) dry white wine

FORCEMEAT STUFFING
40g (1½ ounces) butter
3 medium brown onions (450g), chopped finely
2 rindless bacon slices (130g), chopped coarsely
250g (8 ounces) minced (ground) pork
250g (8 ounces) minced (ground) chicken
1 cup (70g) stale breadcrumbs
½ cup coarsely chopped fresh flat-leaf parsley
½ cup (75g) coarsely chopped roasted unsalted pistachios
2 tablespoons finely chopped fresh tarragon

1 Make forcemeat stuffing.
2 Preheat oven to 180°C/350°F.
3 Discard neck from turkey. Rinse turkey under cold water; pat dry inside and out with absorbent paper. Fill neck cavity loosely with stuffing; secure skin over opening with toothpicks. Fill large cavity loosely with remaining stuffing; tie legs together with kitchen string, tuck wing tips under body.
4 Place turkey on oiled wire rack in large flameproof baking dish; pour the water into dish. Brush turkey all over with half the butter; cover dish tightly with two layers of greased foil. Roast 2 hours. Uncover turkey; brush with remaining butter. Roast, uncovered, about 45 minutes or until turkey is cooked through. Remove turkey from dish, cover; stand 20 minutes.
5 Pour juice from dish into large jug; skim 2 tablespoons of the fat from juice, return fat to same dish. Skim and discard remaining fat from juice. Add flour to dish; cook, stirring, until mixture bubbles and is well browned. Gradually stir in stock, wine and remaining juice; cook, stirring, until gravy boils and thickens. Strain gravy into serving jug or gravy boat.
6 Serve turkey with gravy.

FORCEMEAT STUFFING
Melt butter in medium frying pan; cook onion and bacon, stirring, until onion softens. Cool. Using hand, combine onion mixture in large bowl with remaining ingredients. Season.

To test if turkey is cooked, insert a skewer sideways into the thickest part of the thigh then remove and press flesh to release the juices. If the juice runs clear, the turkey is cooked. Alternatively, insert a meat thermometer into the thickest part of the thigh, without touching the bone; it should reach 90°C/190°F.

ROAST BALSAMIC CHICKEN
with Garlic Bread Sauce

PREP + COOK TIME 1 HOUR 50 MINUTES (+ REFRIGERATION) SERVES 6

1.8kg (3½-pound) whole chicken
⅓ cup (80ml) balsamic vinegar
1 tablespoon dijon mustard
1 tablespoon olive oil
2 sprigs fresh rosemary
500g (1 pound) cherry truss tomatoes
2 sprigs fresh thyme

GARLIC BREAD SAUCE
1¾ cups (430ml) milk
4 cloves garlic, bruised
2 fresh bay leaves
1½ cups (110g) stale breadcrumbs
30g (1 ounce) butter
½ cup (125ml) pouring cream

1 Rinse chicken under cold water. Pat dry inside and out with absorbent paper. Combine vinegar, mustard and oil in large bowl, add chicken; turn to coat chicken in marinade. Cover; refrigerate 3 hours.
2 Preheat oven to 200°C/400°F.
3 Place chicken in large baking dish, reserve marinade. Place one rosemary sprig into chicken cavity. Tie legs together with kitchen string; season. Roast, uncovered, about 1½ hours or until cooked through, basting with reserved marinade. Add tomatoes to dish for last 10 minutes of cooking time.
4 Meanwhile, make garlic bread sauce.
5 Tuck remaining rosemary and thyme between drumsticks; serve chicken with sauce and tomatoes.

GARLIC BREAD SAUCE
Bring milk, garlic and bay leaves to the boil in small saucepan. Remove from heat, stand 30 minutes. Strain milk mixture, discard solids; return milk mixture to same pan. Stir in breadcrumbs and butter; cook, stirring, over low heat, about 10 minutes or until thick. Add cream, stir until heated through; season to taste.

Christmas Eve

SLOW-ROASTED TURKEY
with Wild Rice Seasoning

PREP + COOK TIME 5 HOURS 10 MINUTES **SERVES** 8

4kg (8-pound) turkey
50cm (20-inch) square muslin
100g (3 ounces) butter, melted
1 litre (4 cups) water
40g (1½ ounces) butter
¼ cup (35g) plain (all-purpose) flour
⅓ cup (80ml) port
2 cups (500ml) chicken stock

WILD RICE SEASONING
55g (2 ounces) butter
1 large brown onion (200g), chopped coarsely
2 cloves garlic, crushed
⅓ cup (65g) wild rice
½ cup (125ml) dry white wine
1 cup (250ml) water
⅔ cup (130g) basmati rice
2 cups (500ml) chicken stock
2 medium zucchini (240g), grated coarsely
2 teaspoons finely grated lemon rind
2 teaspoons lemon thyme leaves
1 cup (70g) stale breadcrumbs

1. Make wild rice seasoning.
2. Preheat oven to 150°C/300°F.
3. Discard neck from turkey. Rinse turkey under cold water, pat dry inside and out with absorbent paper. Fill neck cavity loosely with seasoning; secure skin over opening with toothpicks. Fill large cavity loosely with seasoning; tie legs together with kitchen string, tuck wing tips under body.
4. Place turkey on oiled wire rack in large flameproof baking dish. Dip muslin in melted butter and place it over turkey. Pour the water into dish, cover dish with foil. Roast 4 hours.
5. Remove foil and muslin from turkey, brush with pan juices. Increase oven to 200°C/400°F; roast 30 minutes or until turkey is cooked. Remove turkey from dish, cover; stand 20 minutes.
6. Drain pan juices into large jug; skim fat from top, discard. You need 2 cups of pan juices for the gravy.
7. Place baking dish over medium heat, melt butter, add flour; cook, stirring, until well browned. Stir in port, reserved juices and stock; cook, stirring, until gravy boils and thickens. Strain gravy into serving jug or gravy boat.
8. Serve turkey with gravy.

WILD RICE SEASONING
Melt butter in large frying pan; cook onion and garlic, stirring, until onion softens. Add wild rice; cook, stirring, 1 minute. Add wine; simmer, covered, 10 minutes or until almost all the liquid is absorbed. Add the water; simmer, covered, about 10 minutes or until liquid is absorbed. Add basmati rice; cook, stirring, 1 minute. Add stock; simmer, covered, 10 minutes or until all liquid is absorbed and rice is tender. Stir in zucchini, rind and thyme; cool. Add breadcrumbs, season to taste; mix well.

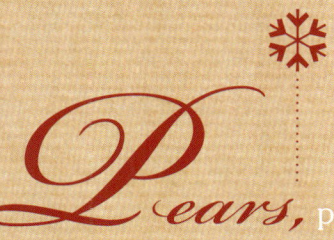

Pears, parsnips and red onion have a natural sweetness that is enhanced on roasting. This sweet flavour balances beautifully with pork's creamy, fatty texture making it the perfect pairing. It's the same reason apple works so well as an accompaniment with pork in all its forms.

ROAST LEG OF PORK
with Pears and Parsnips

PREP + COOK TIME 3 HOURS 15 MINUTES SERVES 8

- 2.5kg (5-pound) boneless pork leg roast, rind on
- 2 tablespoons olive oil
- 1 tablespoon sea salt flakes
- 2 small red onions (200g), quartered
- 2 medium parsnips (500g), quartered
- 4 small firm pears (720g), quartered, cored
- 8 cloves garlic, unpeeled
- ¼ cup (55g) firmly packed light brown sugar
- 2 tablespoons olive oil, extra

1. Preheat oven to 220°C/425°F.
2. Score pork rind with sharp knife; rub with oil then salt. Place pork in large shallow baking dish. Roast, uncovered, 20 minutes.
3. Reduce oven to 180°C/350°F; roast pork, uncovered, a further 2 hours.
4. Meanwhile, combine remaining ingredients in large bowl. Place, in single layer, on oven tray. Roast, uncovered, for last 45 minutes of pork roasting time or until tender. Season to taste.
5. Cover pork loosely with foil; stand 10 minutes before slicing. Serve pork with pear mixture.

ROASTED GOOSE
with Spiced Apples and Onions

PREP + COOK TIME 2 HOURS SERVES 6

3kg (6-pound) goose
1 tablespoon olive oil
6 baby apples (600g), halved
6 pickling onions (240g), halved
1 tablespoon lemon juice
4 sprigs fresh lemon thyme
pinch ground cloves

PISTACHIO AND FIG STUFFING
30g (1 ounce) butter
1 medium red onion (170g), chopped finely
1 large apple (200g), chopped finely
1 stalk celery (150g), trimmed, chopped finely
¼ cup (50g) finely chopped dried figs
¼ cup (35g) pistachios, chopped finely
¼ cup finely chopped fresh flat-leaf parsley

1. Make pistachio and fig stuffing.
2. Preheat oven to 200°C/400°F.
3. Rinse goose under cold water, pat dry inside and out with absorbent paper. Using a small knife, prick goose skin all over. Tuck wings under body. Fill cavity with stuffing. Place wire rack in large, deep baking dish; place goose on rack, season. Roast, uncovered 1½ hours or until cooked through.
4. Meanwhile, heat half the oil in medium frying pan; cook apple, cut-side down, about 5 minutes or until browned lightly.
5. Combine onion, juice, thyme, cloves and remaining oil in small baking dish, add apple; turn to coat apple in mixture, then remove apple from mixture and set aside. Roast onion mixture 45 minutes. Return apples to dish; roast a further 20 minutes or until onions and apples are tender.
6. Serve goose with apple mixture.

PISTACHIO AND FIG STUFFING
Heat butter in medium frying pan; cook onion, apple and celery, stirring, until onion softens. Stir in fig, nuts and parsley. Season to taste; cool.

TURKEY ROLL WITH
Cherry and Almond Stuffing

PREP + COOK TIME 2 HOURS 30 MINUTES (+ STANDING) SERVES 10

3kg (6-pound) double turkey breasts, boned, skin on
20g (¾ ounce) butter, melted
1 tablespoon plain (all-purpose) flour
⅓ cup (80ml) tawny port
¾ cup (180ml) dry white wine
1 cup (250ml) chicken stock
2½ cups (375g) fresh cherries, seeded, quartered

CHERRY AND ALMOND STUFFING
30g (1 ounce) butter
7 shallots (175g), chopped finely
4 cloves garlic, chopped finely
½ cup coarsely chopped fresh marjoram
2 cups (330g) cooked brown rice
1 cup (150g) fresh cherries, seeded, quartered
¼ cup (35g) dried cherries
½ cup (80g) almond kernels, roasted, chopped coarsely
2 eggs

1. Preheat oven to 200°C/400°F.
2. Make cherry and almond stuffing.
3. To butterfly turkey, place breasts, skin-side down, on chopping board; starting from centre of breasts, split one breast in half horizontally, stopping about 1cm (½ inch) from the end, open out flap. Repeat on other side; you should now have one long piece of turkey. Use hands to flatten turkey meat.
4. Place cherry and almond stuffing at one end of turkey; roll up tightly from short side. Use kitchen string to secure at 2.5cm (1-inch) intervals along roll. Brush with butter; season. Place turkey in flameproof dish with enough water to barely cover base of dish. Roast about 1½ hours or until cooked through. Add more water to dish as necessary during cooking to prevent juices burning. To test if turkey is cooked, insert a skewer into the thickest part of the roll; remove skewer and press the flesh. Juices should run clear. Cover roll with foil; stand 20 minutes.
5. Meanwhile, pour pan juices into medium jug; skim fat, return 1 tablespoon of fat to baking dish. Place dish over medium heat; stir in flour, cook, stirring, until well browned. Add port; bring to the boil. Add wine, stock and reserved pan juices; stir until gravy boils and thickens. Add cherries; simmer, uncovered, about 2 minutes or until softened. Season to taste.
6. Serve sliced turkey with gravy.

CHERRY AND ALMOND STUFFING
Melt butter in small frying pan; cook shallot and garlic until browned lightly. Place shallot mixture in large bowl with remaining ingredients; stir to combine. Season.

Order turkey breasts from your butcher and ask him to bone and butterfly them for you. Dried cherries are available from specialty food stores. If unavailable, substitute dried cranberries.
To make shallots easier to peel, pour boiling water over shallots in a heatproof bowl; stand 1 minute. Skins will slip off easily.
You need to cook ⅔ cup brown rice for this recipe.

ROAST PORK LOIN
with Rosemary Gravy

PREP + COOK TIME *2 HOURS* **SERVES** *8*

2kg (4-pound) rolled pork loin
2 teaspoons sea salt flakes
¼ cup (35g) plain (all-purpose) flour
2 tablespoons finely chopped fresh rosemary
½ cup (125ml) dry white wine
2 cups (500ml) chicken stock

CAPSICUM AND CIABATTA CRUMBS
1 tablespoon olive oil
1 medium brown onion (150g), chopped finely
2 cloves garlic, crushed
¼ cup (40g) pine nuts
½ cup (75g) thinly sliced, drained sun-dried tomatoes in oil
½ cup finely chopped drained char-grilled capsicum (bell peppers)
½ cup finely chopped fresh flat-leaf parsley
200g (6½ ounce) piece ciabatta bread, torn into small pieces
½ cup (125ml) chicken stock

1. Make capsicum and ciabatta crumbs.
2. Preheat oven to 240°C/475°F.
3. Cut string from pork; open out pork and place on board, fat-side down. Slice through thickest part of pork horizontally, without cutting all the way through. Open out pork to form one large piece; press capsicum and ciabatta crumbs against loin along width of pork. Roll pork to enclose stuffing, secure with kitchen string at 2cm (¾-inch) intervals.
4. Place pork on rack in large shallow baking dish. Pour enough water into dish to cover base. Rub salt over pork rind. Roast, uncovered, about 30 minutes or until rind is blistered and browned. Reduce oven to 180°C/350°F; roast pork a further 45 minutes or until juices run clear, adding more water to dish if necessary. Remove pork from oven; stand, covered loosely with foil, 10 minutes.
5. Meanwhile, pour juices from dish into large jug; skim one tablespoon of the fat from juices, return fat to dish. Skim and discard remaining fat from juices. Add flour and rosemary to dish; cook, stirring, until mixture bubbles and is well browned. Gradually stir in wine, stock and juices; bring to the boil, stirring, until gravy boils and thickens. Strain gravy into serving jug.
6. Serve sliced pork with gravy.

CAPSICUM AND CIABATTA CRUMBS
Heat oil in large frying pan; cook onion and garlic, stirring, until onion softens. Add nuts; cook, stirring, about 2 minutes or until browned lightly. Stir in remaining ingredients; season to taste, cool.

CORN BREAD
and Candied Sweet Potato Pie
(RECIPE PAGES 82 & 83)

ROAST TURKEY WITH CORN BREAD
and Candied Sweet Potato Pie
(RECIPE PAGES 82 & 83)

ROAST TURKEY WITH CORN BREAD
and Candied Sweet Potato Pie

PREP + COOK TIME 4 HOURS 30 MINUTES (+ STANDING) SERVES 8

4kg (8-pound) turkey
1 cup (250ml) water
45g (1½ ounces) butter, melted
⅓ cup (50g) plain (all-purpose) flour
1 cup (250ml) dry white wine
1 litre (4 cups) chicken stock

CORN BREAD
½ cup (75g) self-raising flour
½ cup (85g) cornmeal
¼ cup (30g) coarsely grated cheddar cheese
125g (4 ounces) canned creamed corn
125g (4 ounces) canned corn kernels, rinsed, drained
⅓ cup (80ml) buttermilk
1 egg, beaten lightly
30g (1 ounce) butter, melted

FORCEMEAT STUFFING
45g (1½ ounces) butter
1 large brown onion (200g), chopped finely
4 thin slices prosciutto (60g), chopped finely
500g (1 pound) minced (ground) chicken
1 cup (70g) stale breadcrumbs
½ cup (60g) coarsely chopped roasted pecans
⅓ cup finely chopped fresh flat-leaf parsley
2 tablespoons finely chopped fresh sage

CANDIED SWEET POTATO PIE
2 large kumara (orange sweet potato) (1kg), chopped coarsely
75g (2½ ounces) butter
2 eggs, beaten lightly
⅓ cup (50g) plain (all-purpose) flour
⅓ cup (75g) firmly packed light brown sugar
½ teaspoon ground cinnamon
¼ teaspoon ground ginger
¾ cup (90g) coarsely chopped roasted pecans

1. Preheat oven to 200°C/400°F; make corn bread.
2. Make forcemeat stuffing.
3. Reduce oven to 180°C/350°F.
4. Fill neck cavity of turkey with some of the stuffing; secure skin with toothpicks or small skewers to enclose stuffing. Fill large cavity with remaining stuffing; secure skin with toothpicks or small skewers. Tie legs together with kitchen string.
5. Place turkey on oiled wire rack in shallow large baking dish; pour the water into dish. Brush turkey all over with butter; season. Roast, covered, 2 hours. Uncover turkey; roast 1 hour, basting occasionally with dish juices, or until turkey is cooked through.
6. Meanwhile, make candied sweet potato pie.
7. Remove turkey from dish; reserve 1/3 cup juices from dish. Cover turkey; stand 20 minutes.
8. Heat reserved juices in same dish. Add flour; cook, stirring, until mixture is well browned. Gradually stir in wine and stock; stir until gravy boils and thickens. Strain gravy into heatproof jug.
9. Serve turkey with gravy, corn bread and candied sweet potato pie.

CORN BREAD
Grease 8cm x 26cm (3¼-inch x 10½-inch) bar cake pan; line base with baking paper, extending paper 5cm (2 inches) over long sides. Sift flour into medium bowl; stir in cornmeal and cheese. Stir in combined remaining ingredients. Spread mixture into pan; bake, about 30 minutes. Stand 10 minutes; turn onto wire rack to cool.

FORCEMEAT STUFFING
Melt butter in medium frying pan; cook onion and prosciutto, stirring, until onion softens. Combine onion mixture in medium bowl with remaining ingredients; season.

CANDIED SWEET POTATO PIE
Boil, steam or microwave kumara until tender; drain. Mash kumara in medium bowl with half of the butter until smooth; stir in egg, season. Spread mixture into oiled 2-litre (8-cup) ovenproof dish. Combine flour, sugar and spices in small bowl; using fingertips, rub in remaining butter. Stir in nuts. Sprinkle nut mixture over kumara; bake, uncovered, about 30 minutes or until browned.

(PHOTOGRAPH PAGES 80 & 81)

THE STOCKINGS WERE HUNG
by the Chimney with Care

KIDS LOOK FORWARD to Christmas morning
to discover all the treats in their stocking.
Selecting stocking fillers is a universal **JOY OF PARENTS** at Christmas.
If you don't have a fireplace get creative and
HANG THE STOCKINGS from a coat hook or hallstand.
You will need Christmas stockings **FOR EVERY CHILD**
and a variety of small presents.
LOOP THE STOCKING around the hooks
on a stand or coat hook to secure them
and fill with individually wrapped
small presents.

PORK RACK
with Sage Apples

PORK RACK
with Sage Apples
PREP + COOK TIME *1 HOUR 10 MINUTES* **SERVES 6**

1kg (2-pound) rack of pork (6 cutlets), rind on
1 tablespoon olive oil
1 tablespoon sea salt flakes
1.25kg (2½ pounds) kipfler potatoes
750g (1½ pounds) pumpkin, chopped coarsely
SAGE APPLES
3 large green apples (600g)
¼ cup (60ml) water
4 fresh sage leaves
1 teaspoon white (granulated) sugar

1. Preheat oven to 220ºC/425ºF.
2. Rub pork rind with half the oil then the salt. Stand pork in medium baking dish; roast, uncovered, about 35 minutes or until rind is blistered.
3. Place vegetables in baking dish with pork, drizzle with remaining oil. Reduce oven to 180ºC/350ºF.
4. Roast pork and vegetables, uncovered, about 40 minutes or until pork is cooked through. Remove pork from dish; cover to keep warm.
5. Increase oven to 220ºC/425ºF; roast vegetables a further 15 minutes.
6. Meanwhile, make sage apples.
7. Serve pork with vegetables and sage apples.

SAGE APPLES
Peel and core apples; slice thickly. Place apple, the water and sage in medium saucepan; simmer, uncovered, about 10 minutes or until apple is soft. Remove from heat, stir in sugar.

GLAZED CARROTS
with Hazelnuts
PREP + COOK TIME *25 MINUTES* **SERVES 4 (AS A SIDE)**

30g (1 ounce) butter
800g (1½ pounds) baby carrots, trimmed, peeled
2 teaspoons finely grated orange rind
¼ cup (60ml) orange juice
2 tablespoons dry white wine
2 tablespoons pure maple syrup
½ cup (70g) coarsely chopped roasted hazelnuts

1. Melt butter in large frying pan; cook carrots, turning occasionally, about 5 minutes or until almost tender. Add rind, juice, wine and syrup; bring to the boil. Reduce heat; simmer, uncovered, until liquid has almost evaporated and carrots are tender and caramelised. Season to taste.
2. Serve carrots sprinkled with nuts.

(PHOTOGRAPH PAGE 88)

GLAZED CARROTS
with Hazelnuts
(RECIPE PAGE 87)

BRUSSELS SPROUTS
with Crispy Onions and Pancetta
(RECIPE PAGE 90)

BRUSSELS SPROUTS WITH
Crispy Onions and Pancetta

PREP + COOK TIME 25 MINUTES SERVES 8

750g (1½ pounds) brussels sprouts, halved
30g (1 ounce) butter
1 tablespoon olive oil
1 large brown onion (200g), sliced thinly
6 slices pancetta (90g), sliced thinly
2 cloves garlic, sliced thinly
¼ cup finely chopped fresh flat-leaf parsley

1. Boil, steam or microwave sprouts until barely tender; drain.
2. Meanwhile, heat butter and oil in large frying pan. Add onion, pancetta and garlic; cook, stirring, about 10 minutes or until onion starts to caramelise and pancetta is crisp. Add sprouts; cook, stirring, until heated through. Season to taste.
3. Serve sprouts sprinkled with parsley.

(PHOTOGRAPH PAGE 89)

ASPARAGUS SALAD WITH SPRING ONION
and Pea Vinaigrette

PREP + COOK TIME 40 MINUTES SERVES 6

1 cup (250ml) dry white wine
1 teaspoon sugar
8 spring onions (200g), trimmed, sliced thinly
1½ cups (180g) frozen peas
500g (1 pound) asparagus, trimmed
1 tablespoon olive oil

1. Bring wine and sugar to the boil in medium frying pan. Reduce heat; simmer, uncovered until mixture is reduced to about ¼ cup.
2. Meanwhile, half-fill another medium frying pan with water, add a little salt; bring to the boil. Drop onion into the boiling water, cook 30 seconds; remove with a slotted spoon to a strainer. Rinse under cold water; drain.
3. Using the same boiling water, repeat with peas then asparagus. Place asparagus on serving platter.
4. Add oil to wine mixture with onion and peas; heat gently over low heat, season; pour over asparagus.

Serve salad warm or at room temperature.

ASPARAGUS SALAD WITH SPRING ONION
and Pea Vinaigrette

HASSELBACK
Potatoes

HASSELBACK
Potatoes

PREP + COOK TIME 1 HOUR 30 MINUTES **SERVES** 4

4 medium potatoes (800g), halved
40g (1½ ounces) butter, melted
2 tablespoons olive oil
¼ cup (25g) packaged breadcrumbs
½ cup (940g) finely grated parmesan cheese

1. Preheat oven to 180°C/350°F. Place potatoes, cut-side down, on chopping board; working with one half at a time, place a chopstick on board along each side of potato. Slice potato thinly, cutting through to chopsticks to prevent cutting all the way through. Repeat with remaining potatoes.
2. Combine butter and oil in medium baking dish; add potatoes, turn to coat. Place, rounded-side up, in single layer; roast 1 hour, brushing often with oil mixture.
3. Combine breadcrumbs and cheese in small bowl; sprinkle over potatoes. Roast about 10 minutes or until browned.

DOUBLE CHEESE
Potato Gratin

PREP + COOK TIME 1 HOUR 35 MINUTES (+ STANDING) **SERVES** 8

1¼ cups (310ml) pouring cream
1 cup (250ml) milk
50g (1½ ounces) butter
¼ teaspoon ground nutmeg
3 sprigs fresh thyme
2 cloves garlic, bruised
1.5kg (3 pounds) potatoes
1 cup (120g) coarsely grated smoked cheddar cheese
½ cup (40g) coarsely grated parmesan cheese

1. Heat cream, milk, butter, nutmeg, thyme and garlic in medium saucepan until just below boiling point. Stand 15 minutes. Discard thyme and garlic.
2. Meanwhile, preheat oven to 200°C/400°F. Grease 2-litre (8-cup) shallow ovenproof dish.
3. Using V-slicer or mandoline, slice potatoes thinly. Layer potato and cheddar in dish; pour over cream mixture. Cover dish with greased foil, bake 45 minutes.
4. Remove foil, top with parmesan; bake, uncovered, 20 minutes or until potato is tender and browned.

It is fine to use just one 300ml carton of cream for this recipe.

(PHOTOGRAPH PAGE 94)

DOUBLE CHEESE
Potato Gratin
(RECIPE PAGE 93)

TOMATO BASIL
and Pine Nut Salad

(RECIPE PAGE 96)

TOMATO BASIL
and Pine Nut Salad

PREP TIME 30 MINUTES **SERVES** 8 (AS A SIDE)

1kg (2 pounds) assorted tomatoes
¼ cup lightly packed small fresh basil leaves
BASIL AND PINE NUT DRESSING
½ cup firmly packed fresh basil leaves
¼ cup (40g) pine nuts, roasted
1 clove garlic, quartered
⅓ cup (80ml) olive oil
1½ teaspoons red wine vinegar

1. Make basil and pine nut dressing.
2. Roughly chop or halve tomatoes, combine in serving bowl; season. Drizzle with dressing; sprinkle with basil.

BASIL AND PINE NUT DRESSING
Blend or process basil, nuts and garlic until chopped coarsely. With motor operating, gradually add oil; process until chopped finely. Stir in vinegar.

Use an assortment of tomatoes in season to make a bright summery salad. We used a mixture of ox heart, egg (plum), cherry, yellow teardrop and black tomatoes.

(PHOTOGRAPH PAGE 95)

ROASTED ROSEMARY
and Pepper Beets

PREP + COOK TIME 1 HOUR 10 MINUTES **SERVES** 8

2kg (4 pounds) baby beetroot (beets)
4 fresh rosemary sprigs
8 cloves garlic, unpeeled
½ teaspoon cracked black pepper
¼ cup (60ml) olive oil
1 tablespoon lemon juice

1. Preheat oven to 200°C/400°F.
2. Trim ends of beetroot, leaving 2cm (¾ inch) of the stem attached; halve beetroot if large. Reserve small unblemished beetroot leaves.
3. Combine beetroot, rosemary, garlic, pepper and 2 tablespoons of the oil in large baking dish; season. Roast, uncovered, about 45 minutes or until beetroot are tender.
4. Squeeze garlic flesh from skins; chop garlic finely. Combine garlic, juice and remaining oil in small bowl; season to taste. Place beetroot and reserved leaves on serving platter; drizzle with garlic mixture.

Christmas Eve

ROASTED ROSEMARY
and Pepper Beets

PEAR AND
Witlof Salad

PEAR AND *Witlof Salad*

PREP TIME 15 MINUTES SERVES 6

6 small witlof (belgian endive) (750g), leaves separated
350g (11 ounces) watercress, trimmed
2 small pears (360g), quartered, cored, sliced thinly
1 cup (110g) coarsely chopped roasted walnuts
100g (3 ounces) creamy blue cheese, crumbled

MUSTARD DRESSING
2 tablespoons olive oil
1 tablespoon red wine vinegar
1 teaspoon dijon mustard
1 teaspoon light brown sugar

1 Make mustard dressing.
2 Place witlof, watercress and pear in large bowl with nuts; add dressing, toss to combine. Divide salad between serving plates; sprinkle with cheese.

MUSTARD DRESSING
Place ingredients in screw-top jar; shake well. Season to taste.

BROAD BEANS *and Thyme*

PREP + COOK TIME 40 MINUTES SERVES 6 (AS A SIDE)

600g (1¼ pounds) frozen broad beans (fava beans), thawed
10g (½ ounce) butter
2 shallots (50g), chopped finely
150g (4½ ounces) speck, chopped finely
1 tablespoon fresh thyme leaves
1 tablespoon lemon juice

1 Drop beans into medium saucepan of boiling water, return to the boil; drain. When beans are cool enough to handle, peel away grey-coloured outer shells.
2 Heat butter in large frying pan; cook shallot and speck, stirring, until speck is browned lightly. Add beans and thyme; cook, stirring, until beans are heated through. Stir in juice; season to taste.

(PHOTOGRAPH PAGE 100)

BROAD BEANS
and Thyme
(RECIPE PAGE 99)

ROASTED VEGETABLES WITH
Garlic and Coriander Oil

(RECIPE PAGE 102)

ROASTED VEGETABLES WITH
Garlic and Coriander Oil

PREP + COOK TIME 1 HOUR 10 MINUTES (+ STANDING) **SERVES** 8

⅓ cup (80ml) olive oil
4 cloves garlic, bruised
2 teaspoons fennel seeds, crushed
2 teaspoons coriander seeds, crushed
12 baby new potatoes (480g), halved
4 small parsnips (480g), quartered lengthways
400g (12½ ounces) baby carrots, trimmed
2 small red capsicum (bell peppers) (300g), sliced thickly
1 large red onion (300g), cut into wedges

1 Preheat oven to 200°C/400°F. Line two oven trays with baking paper.
2 Heat oil, garlic and seeds in small saucepan over low heat. Remove from heat; stand 30 minutes.
3 Divide vegetables between trays. Strain oil over vegetables; discard solids. Turn vegetables to coat; season. Roast, uncovered, about 50 minutes or until vegetables are browned and tender.

(PHOTOGRAPH PAGE 101)

ROASTED CARAMELISED
Parsnips

PREP + COOK TIME 1 HOUR 10 MINUTES **SERVES** 4 (AS A SIDE)

1kg (2 pounds) parsnips, halved lengthways
2 tablespoons olive oil
¼ cup (55g) firmly packed light brown sugar
1 teaspoon ground nutmeg
1 tablespoon finely chopped fresh flat-leaf parsley

1 Preheat oven to 220°C/425°F.
2 Combine parsnips, oil, sugar and nutmeg in large shallow baking dish; season. Roast, uncovered, about 1 hour or until browned and tender.
3 Serve parsnips sprinkled with parsley.

ROASTED CARAMELISED
Parsnips

CHAPTER 3
Christmas
MORNING

DECK THE HALLS
✱ with Boughs of Holly ✱

A HALLWAY CAN BE TRANSFORMED
by hanging some beautiful baubles
from an existing CHANDELIER OR LAMPSHADE.
YOU WILL NEED a minimum of 10 baubles of your choice,
a selection of coloured ribbon, scissors and masking tape.
FOR A CHANDELIER – cut the ribbon into lengths and thread each bauble
with ribbon (each ribbon can be a different length) leaving the ends untied.
Using a stepladder to safely REACH THE CHANDELIER
carefully loop the ribbon around each arm of the chandelier
and tie into a knot allowing each bauble to HANG FREELY.
FOR A LAMPSHADE – cut ribbon into lengths and tie one end to each bauble.
Using a stepladder to safely reach the lampshade
attach the other END OF THE RIBBON
to the inside of the lampshade.
FIX IN PLACE with masking tape, pressing down well to
secure in place.

GREEN GRAPE
and Apple Spritzer
PREP TIME 10 MINUTES SERVES 4

Using an electric juicer, extract juice from 500g (1 pound) seedless green grapes and 1 coarsely chopped large apple. Combine with 2 cups chilled soda water and 1 thinly sliced lime in large jug.

APPLE, PEAR
and Cranberry Juice
PREP TIME 10 MINUTES SERVES 2

Using an electric juicer, extract juice from 2 coarsely chopped large apples, 2 coarsely chopped small pears and 1 cup thawed, frozen cranberries.

GINGER, ORANGE
and Pineapple Juice
PREP TIME 5 MINUTES SERVES 1

Juice 1 medium orange on citrus squeezer; pour into glass. Blend or process 200g (6½ ounces) (about ¼ small) coarsely chopped pineapple and 2cm (¾-inch) piece fresh ginger until smooth. Stir into orange juice.

PINEAPPLE, CARROT
and Beetroot Juice
PREP TIME 5 MINUTES SERVES 1

Using an electric juicer, extract juice from ¼ small thickly sliced pineapple, 2 medium carrots and 1 small beetroot (beet) into glass. Stir in 2 tablespoons water and 1 tablespoon lime juice.

BERRY AND YOGURT
Muffin

GLAZED FIG
Bruschetta

BERRY AND YOGURT *Muffins*

PREP + COOK TIME 35 MINUTES MAKES 6

1½ cups (225g) self-raising flour
⅓ cup (30g) rolled oats
3 eggs
¾ cup (165g) firmly packed light brown sugar
¾ cup (200g) yogurt
⅓ cup (80ml) vegetable oil
180g (5½ ounces) fresh or frozen mixed berries

1. Preheat oven to 200°C/400°F. Grease six-hole (¾-cup/180ml) texas muffin pan.
2. Sift flour into medium bowl; stir in oats, eggs, sugar, yogurt and oil, then berries. Do not over-mix. Spoon mixture into pan holes.
3. Bake muffins about 25 minutes. Stand muffins in pan 5 minutes; turn, top-side up, onto wire rack to cool.
4. Serve muffins dusted with a little sifted icing (confectioners') sugar.

GLAZED FIG *Bruschetta*

PREP + COOK TIME 10 MINUTES SERVES 4

6 medium fresh figs (360g), halved
2 tablespoons honey
1 tablespoon cold water
⅔ cup (160ml) thickened (heavy) cream
1 tablespoon icing (confectioners') sugar
⅓ cup (85g) mascarpone cheese
4 thick slices brioche (200g), toasted

1. Drizzle cut-sides of figs with honey. Place figs, cut-side down, in heated large frying pan; cook until warmed through. Add the water to pan; remove from heat.
2. Meanwhile, beat cream and sugar in small bowl with electric mixer until soft peaks form. Beat in cheese.
3. Spread one side of each brioche with cheese mixture; top with fig halves.

Christmas Morning

PORRIDGE WITH BANANA
and Brazil Nuts

PREP + COOK TIME 10 MINUTES SERVES 4

2 cups (500ml) water
1 cup (250ml) milk
1⅓ cups (120g) rolled oats
2 medium bananas (400g), sliced thickly
⅓ cup (55g) roasted brazil nuts, sliced thinly
1 tablespoon honey
1⅓ cups (330ml) milk, extra

1. Bring the water and milk to the boil in medium saucepan. Reduce heat; add oats. Simmer, stirring, about 5 minutes or until porridge is thick and creamy.
2. Serve porridge topped with banana, nuts, honey and extra milk.

BANANA MAPLE PANCAKES
with Pecans

PREP + COOK TIME 20 MINUTES SERVES 4

½ cup (75g) self-raising flour
1 tablespoon caster (superfine) sugar
⅔ cup (160ml) buttermilk
1 egg white
2 tablespoons pure maple syrup
10g (½ ounce) butter, melted
1 medium banana (200g), sliced thinly
¼ cup (60ml) pure maple syrup, extra
¼ cup (30g) roasted pecans, chopped coarsely

1. Sift flour and sugar into medium bowl; whisk in buttermilk, egg white, syrup and butter until mixture is smooth. Stir in banana.
2. Pour ¼ cup of the batter into heated oiled large frying pan. Cook, uncovered, until bubbles appear on surface. Turn; cook until browned lightly. Remove from pan; cover to keep warm. Repeat process with remaining batter to make a total of eight pancakes.
3. Serve pancakes drizzled with extra syrup then sprinkled with nuts.

PORRIDGE
WITH BANANA
and Brazil Nuts

BANANA
MAPLE PANCAKES
with Pecans

Christmas Day can be hectic for everyone with present-opening at dawn and lunch with the in-laws. Before you go, start the day with a light luxury breakfast and invite loved ones en route to their Christmas lunch.

POTATO PANCAKES WITH SMOKED SALMON
and Dill Cream

PREP + COOK TIME 50 *MINUTES* **SERVES** 8

3 medium unpeeled potatoes (600g)
1 medium brown onion (150g), grated coarsely
2 eggs, beaten lightly
¼ cup (35g) self-raising flour
2 tablespoons olive oil
125g (4 ounces) crème fraîche
1½ tablespoons finely chopped fresh dill
1½ tablespoons lime juice
200g (6½ ounces) sliced smoked salmon
2 cups (230g) firmly packed trimmed watercress
2 tablespoons salmon roe

1. Place whole potatoes in medium saucepan, barely cover with cold water; cover pan, bring to the boil. Reduce heat, simmer, covered, about 20 minutes or until tender. Drain. When cool enough to handle, peel potatoes. Grate coarsely into large bowl.
2. Stir onion, eggs and flour into potato; season.
3. Heat oil in large frying pan. Drop 2 tablespoons of mixture into pan, making each pancake about 5cm (2 inches) in diameter. Cook about 3 minutes each side or until pancakes are browned lightly. Drain on absorbent paper.
4. Meanwhile, combine crème fraîche, dill and juice in small bowl.
5. Place pancakes on serving plates; top with salmon, dill cream, watercress and salmon roe. Sprinkle with a little extra dill.

MASALA
Omelette

MASALA
Omelette

PREP + COOK TIME 30 MINUTES SERVES 4

10 eggs
½ cup (125ml) milk
⅔ cup (80g) coarsely grated cheddar cheese
30g (1 ounce) butter
1 medium tomato (150g), seeded, chopped finely
¼ small red onion (25g), chopped finely
1 fresh long green chilli, chopped finely
½ small green capsicum (bell pepper) (75g), chopped finely
½ cup loosely packed fresh coriander (cilantro) leaves

1 Beat eggs, milk and cheese with fork in large bowl until combined; season.
2 Combine tomato, onion, chilli and capsicum in small bowl.
3 Melt a quarter of the butter in small non-stick frying pan; pour a quarter of the egg mixture into pan. Cook omelette until almost set; sprinkle with a quarter of the tomato mixture. Fold omelette over; slide onto heated plate, cover to keep warm. Repeat with remaining butter, egg mixture and tomato mixture to make another three omelettes.
4 Serve omelettes sprinkled with coriander.

POACHED EGGS
with Lemon Asparagus

PREP + COOK TIME 35 MINUTES SERVES 4

4 eggs
350g (11 ounces) asparagus
2 tablespoons lemon juice
¼ cup (20g) finely grated parmesan cheese
¼ cup (20g) flaked parmesan cheese

1 To poach eggs, half-fill large shallow frying pan with water; bring to the boil. Break one egg into a cup, then slide into pan; repeat with three more eggs. When all eggs are in pan, allow water to return to the boil. Cover pan, turn off heat; stand about 4 minutes or until a light film of egg white sets over yolks. Using a slotted spoon, remove eggs one at a time from pan; drain on absorbent paper, cover to keep warm.
2 Meanwhile, cook asparagus on heated oiled grill plate (or grill or barbecue) about 3 minutes or until tender. Place asparagus in large bowl, add juice and grated parmesan; toss gently. Season to taste.
3 Divide asparagus among serving plates; top with poached eggs, flaked parmesan and freshly ground black pepper.

(PHOTOGRAPH PAGE 118)

POACHED EGGS
with Lemon Asparagus
(RECIPE PAGE 117)

BAKED Eggs
(RECIPE PAGE 120)

BAKED *Eggs*

PREP + COOK TIME 25 MINUTES SERVES 4

1 tablespoon olive oil
100g (3 ounces) prosciutto, chopped finely
100g (3 ounces) button mushrooms, chopped finely
4 green onions (scallions), chopped finely
100g (3 ounces) slightly underripe brie cheese, chopped coarsely
8 eggs

1. Preheat oven to 200°C/400°F. Oil four ¾-cup (180ml) shallow ovenproof dishes.
2. Heat oil in medium frying pan; cook prosciutto, mushrooms and onion, stirring, until onion softens. Remove from heat; stir in half the cheese. Divide prosciutto mixture between dishes; carefully break two eggs into each dish.
3. Bake eggs 5 minutes; increase oven to 220°C/425°F.
4. Sprinkle remaining cheese over eggs; bake about 5 minutes or until eggs set and cheese melts.

This is the perfect brunch dish for entertaining, as you don't have to stand over it while it cooks. Sprinkle chopped fresh parsley over the top of the baked eggs to add colour and flavour.

(PHOTOGRAPH PAGE 119)

APPLE *Turnovers*

PREP + COOK TIME 40 MINUTES MAKES 36

1 cup (225g) canned apple pie filling
¼ cup (40g) dried currants
2 tablespoons light brown sugar
¼ teaspoon mixed spice
4 sheets puff pastry
1 egg, beaten lightly
2 teaspoons demerara sugar

1. Preheat oven to 220°C/425°F. Grease two oven trays; line with baking paper.
2. Combine apple pie filling, currants, brown sugar and spice in medium bowl.
3. Cut nine 8cm (3¼-inch) circles from each pastry sheet; top circles with rounded teaspoons of apple mixture. Fold to enclose filling; pinch edges to seal.
4. Place turnovers on tray, brush with egg; sprinkle with demerara sugar.
5. Bake turnovers 20 minutes or until golden brown.

You can make the turnovers up to step 4 and freeze in an airtight container. Brush frozen turnovers with egg, sprinkle with sugar and bake about 25 minutes.

Christmas Morning

APPLE
Turnovers

ECCLES MINCE Pies

PREP + COOK TIME *1 HOUR (+ REFRIGERATION)* **MAKES 63**

7 sheets puff pastry
1 egg white, beaten lightly
1½ tablespoons white (granulated) sugar
FRUIT MINCE
1 cup (150g) raisins
1 cup (160g) dried currants
1 cup (160g) sultanas
1 slice (35g) dried pineapple
2 tablespoons glacé cherries
¼ cup (40g) blanched almonds
1 large apple (200g), grated coarsely
½ cup (110g) lightly packed light brown sugar
50g (1½ ounces) butter, melted
1 tablespoon finely grated orange rind
¼ cup (60ml) orange juice
¼ cup (60ml) brandy
½ teaspoon mixed spice

1. Make fruit mince.
2. Preheat oven to 200°C/400°F. Line three oven trays with baking paper.
3. Cut each pastry sheet into nine squares. Top each with heaped teaspoons of fruit mince; brush pastry edges with egg white. Gather sides of pastry together to encase filling; turn pies upside down onto trays. Gently flatten pies; cut two slits in top of pies. Brush pies with egg white; sprinkle with sugar.
4. Bake pies 15 minutes or until golden brown.

FRUIT MINCE
Process dried fruit and nuts until coarsely chopped. Transfer mixture to large bowl; stir in remaining ingredients. Refrigerate, covered, at least 2 days, stirring daily.

Fruit mince will keep for at least a year in an airtight container in the refrigerator. The flavours will intensify the longer it is left before using. This recipe makes 3½ cups of fruit mince; you can use ready-made fruit mince if you're running out of time. You can fill and shape the pies, and freeze in an airtight container for up to 2 months. Brush frozen pies with egg white, sprinkle with sugar and bake about 20 minutes.

CUSTARD FRUIT *Flans*

PREP + COOK TIME 1 HOUR (+ REFRIGERATION & COOLING) MAKES 24

1¾ cups (260g) plain (all-purpose) flour
¼ cup (40g) icing (confectioners') sugar
185g (6 ounces) cold butter, chopped coarsely
1 egg yolk
2 teaspoons iced water, approximately
1 medium kiwifruit (85g)
60g (2 ounces) fresh raspberries, halved
60g (2 ounces) fresh blueberries

CUSTARD CREAM
1 cup (250ml) milk
1 teaspoon vanilla extract
3 egg yolks
⅓ cup (75g) caster (superfine) sugar
2 tablespoons pure cornflour (cornstarch)
⅓ cup (80ml) thickened (heavy) cream, whipped

1. Process flour, sugar and butter until crumbly. With motor operating, add egg yolk and enough of the water to make ingredients come together. Turn dough onto floured surface, knead gently until smooth. Wrap pastry in plastic; refrigerate 30 minutes.
2. Grease two 12-hole (1-tablespoon/20ml) mini muffin pans. Roll out half the pastry between sheets of baking paper until 3mm (⅛-inch) thick. Cut 12 x 6cm (2¼-inch) rounds from pastry; press rounds into holes of one pan. Prick bases of cases well with a fork. Repeat with remaining pastry. Refrigerate 30 minutes.
3. Preheat oven to 220°C/425°F.
4. Bake cases about 12 minutes. Stand cases in pan 5 minutes, before transferring to wire rack to cool.
5. Meanwhile, make custard cream.
6. Cut kiwifruit crossways into eight slices; cut 3cm (1¼-inch) rounds from slices. Divide custard cream into cases; top with fruit.

CUSTARD CREAM
Bring milk and extract to the boil in small saucepan. Meanwhile, beat egg yolks, sugar and cornflour in small bowl with electric mixer until thick. With motor operating, gradually beat in hot milk mixture. Return custard to pan; stir over heat until mixture boils and thickens. Cover surface of custard with plastic wrap, refrigerate 1 hour. Fold cream into custard, in two batches.

Pastry cases and custard cream can be made and stored separately, 2 days ahead; fold cream into custard just before using. Assemble flans as close to serving time as possible – about an hour is good.

Christmas Morning

CHAMPAGNE *Cocktail*

PREP TIME 5 MINUTES SERVES 6

6 sugar cubes
12 drops angostura bitters
3 cups (750ml) chilled champagne
2 x 10cm (4-inch) strips orange rind, sliced thinly

1 Place one sugar cube in each champagne glass; top with bitters then champagne. Garnish with rind.

BELLINI

PREP TIME 5 MINUTES SERVES 8

2 medium peaches (300g), chopped coarsely
½ cup (125ml) peach schnapps
3 cups (750ml) chilled champagne
8 sugar cubes

1 Blend or process peach and schnapps until smooth; combine with champagne in large jug.
2 Place one sugar cube in each champagne glass; top with bellini mixture.

LEMON, LIME *and Bitters Punch*

PREP TIME 10 MINUTES (+ REFRIGERATION) SERVES 8

5 lemon infusion tea bags
1 litre (4 cups) boiling water
1.25 litres (5 cups) lemonade
¼ cup (60ml) lime juice cordial
1 teaspoon angostura bitters
3 cups ice cubes
2 limes, sliced thinly

1 Combine tea bags and the water in large heatproof jug; stand 5 minutes. Discard tea bags; cool tea to room temperature then refrigerate until cold.
2 Just before serving, add remaining ingredients to jug; stir to combine.

EGGNOG

PREP + COOK TIME 25 MINUTES (+ REFRIGERATION) SERVES 8

4 eggs, separated
⅓ cup (75g) caster (superfine) sugar
2 cups (500ml) hot milk
½ cup (125ml) brandy
½ cup (125ml) thickened (heavy) cream

1 Place egg yolks, sugar and milk in large heatproof bowl over a saucepan of simmering water (don't allow water to touch base of bowl). Whisk about 15 minutes or until mixture lightly coats the back of a metal spoon. Remove from heat, stir in brandy, cover; refrigerate 1 hour.
2 Beat cream in small bowl until soft peaks form; fold into liqueur mixture.
3 Beat egg whites in small bowl with electric mixer until soft peaks form; gently fold into liqueur mixture, in two batches.

MELON, BOCCONCINI
and Mint Salad

PREP TIME 20 MINUTES MAKES 12

Make balls from half a rockmelon and honeydew melon; combine in colander with 200g (6½ ounces) cherry bocconcini cheese and ¼ cup torn fresh mint leaves. Place colander on tray or inside large bowl; refrigerate until ready to serve. Combine 2 teaspoons each extra virgin olive oil and lemon juice in small bowl; season to taste. Just before serving, place melon mixture in large bowl with 30g (1 ounce) torn prosciutto and dressing; toss gently to combine. Spoon salad into twelve ⅔-cup (160ml) glasses.

TOMATO, BASIL
and Pasta Salad

PREP + COOK TIME 15 MINUTES MAKES 12

Cook 1½ cups small pasta shells in boiling water until tender; rinse under cold water, drain. Place pasta in large bowl with 250g (8 ounces) halved cherry tomatoes and ⅓ cup shredded fresh basil. Combine 2 tablespoons extra virgin olive oil, 1 tablespoon lemon juice, ½ crushed garlic clove and 2 finely chopped anchovies in small bowl; season to taste. Pour dressing over salad; toss gently to combine. Spoon salad into twelve ⅔-cup (160ml) glasses; top with extra basil.

STRAWBERRY AND
Smoked Salmon Salad

PREP TIME 15 MINUTES MAKES 12

Combine 250g (8 ounces) quartered, hulled small strawberries, 100g (3 ounces) chopped sliced smoked salmon and 40g (1½ ounces) baby rocket (arugula) leaves in large bowl; refrigerate until ready to serve. Meanwhile, combine 1 tablespoon extra virgin olive oil and 2 teaspoons white balsamic dressing in small bowl; season to taste. Just before serving, add dressing to salad; toss gently. Spoon salad into twelve ⅔-cup (160ml) glasses.

BROAD BEAN,
Pine Nut and Rocket Salad

PREP + COOK TIME 30 MINUTES MAKES 12

Cook 3 cups frozen broad beans (fava beans) in boiling water about 2 minutes; drain. Cool in iced water; drain. Peel away grey-coloured outer shells. Combine beans with ¼ cup roasted pine nuts, 40g (1½ ounces) coarsely chopped baby rocket (arugula) leaves and 1 tablespoon coarsely grated parmesan cheese in large bowl; refrigerate. Meanwhile, combine 1 tablespoon extra virgin olive oil, 2 teaspoons lemon juice and ½ crushed garlic clove in small bowl; season to taste. Just before serving, add dressing to salad; toss gently to combine. Spoon salad into twelve ⅔-cup (160ml) glasses; top with small basil leaves and flaked parmesan cheese.

MARINATED DUCK
with Peppered Strawberries

PREP + COOK TIME 45 MINUTES (+ REFRIGERATION) SERVES 6

¾ cup (225g) rock salt
¾ cup (165g) firmly packed light brown sugar
2 tablespoons sichuan pepper
4 x 220g (7-ounce) duck breasts
70g (2½ ounces) baby rocket (arugula) leaves

PEPPERED STRAWBERRIES
250g (8 ounces) strawberries, hulled, halved
½ teaspoon each ground white pepper and finely cracked black pepper
¼ cup (60ml) olive oil
1½ cups (225g) cherries, seeded, halved
2 tablespoons balsamic vinegar
1 tablespoon finely grated orange rind
2 tablespoons orange juice
2 shallots (50g) chopped finely

1. Combine rock salt, sugar and pepper in large bowl, add duck breasts; turn to coat. Cover; refrigerate 3 hours.
2. Brush off marinade; pat duck dry with absorbent paper. Place duck, skin-side down, in lightly oiled heated large frying pan; cook, over low heat, about 20 minutes or until skin is browned. Turn duck; cook about 4 minutes or until cooked to your liking. Remove duck from pan, cover loosely with foil; stand 10 minutes before slicing thickly.
3. Meanwhile, make peppered strawberries.
4. Serve duck on rocket with strawberries.

PEPPERED STRAWBERRIES
Combine berries, peppers and 1 tablespoon of the oil in medium bowl. Cook strawberry mixture on heated grill plate (or grill or barbecue) for 30 seconds. Transfer to medium bowl; cool. Stir in cherries, vinegar, rind, juice, shallot and remaining oil.

Duck breasts are available from poultry shops and some butcher shops.

ONION, THYME AND *Goat's Cheese Tarts*

PREP + COOK TIME 1 HOUR 20 MINUTES (+ REFRIGERATION) MAKES 6

1½ cups (225g) plain (all-purpose) flour
1½ tablespoons fresh thyme leaves
125g (4 ounces) cold butter, chopped coarsely
1 egg yolk
2 tablespoons iced water
1 tablespoon olive oil
2 large brown onions (400g), sliced thinly
3 eggs
⅔ cup (160ml) pouring cream
125g (4 ounces) goat's cheese, sliced into six rounds

1. Process flour, 1 tablespoon of the thyme and butter until mixture is crumbly. Add egg yolk and the water; process until ingredients come together. Enclose in plastic wrap; refrigerate 30 minutes.
2. Grease six 3cm (1¼-inch) deep x 8cm (3¼-inch) round loose-based flan tins. Divide pastry into six equal pieces. Roll one piece between sheets of baking paper until large enough to line tin. Lift pastry into tin, press into side; trim edge. Repeat with remaining pastry. Cover; refrigerate 20 minutes.
3. Preheat oven to 200°C/400°F. Place tins on oven tray; cover pastry with baking paper, fill with dried beans or rice. Bake 15 minutes. Remove paper and beans; bake about 10 minutes or until browned lightly. Cool.
4. Meanwhile, heat oil in large frying pan; cook onion, stirring, about 15 minutes or until caramelised. Place onion in pastry cases.
5. Whisk eggs and cream in large jug, season; pour into pastry cases. Top with cheese, sprinkle with remaining thyme.
6. Bake tarts about 25 minutes or until barely set.
7. Serve tarts topped with baby rocket (arugula) and accompany with a green leaf salad, if you like.

CHARCUTERIE
Plate

PREP + COOK TIME 45 MINUTES SERVES 10

1 tablespoon finely chopped fresh tarragon
2 tablespoons olive oil
24 cherry tomatoes (250g)
1 loaf sourdough bread (675g), sliced thickly
150g (4½ ounces) thinly sliced prosciutto
150g (4½ ounces) thinly sliced salami
150g (4½ ounces) thinly sliced pastrami
120g (4 ounces) chicken liver pâté

PICKLED MUSHROOMS
2 tablespoons olive oil
50g (1½ ounces) shiitake mushrooms, trimmed
70g (2½ ounces) swiss brown mushrooms, quartered
100g (3 ounces) enoki mushrooms, trimmed
3 fresh small red thai (serrano) chillies
4 sprigs fresh thyme
1 tablespoon caster (superfine) sugar
2 tablespoons sherry vinegar

CARROT AND TURMERIC SALAD
1 large carrot (180g), cut into matchsticks
¾ cup (225g) mayonnaise
2 teaspoons finely grated lime rind
2 teaspoons lime juice
1 teaspoon ground turmeric
1 teaspoon yellow mustard seeds, toasted
2 tablespoons finely chopped fresh chives

1 Make pickled mushrooms; make carrot and turmeric salad.
2 Combine tarragon and oil in medium bowl; season to taste. Add tomatoes; toss gently to combine.
3 Char-grill or toast sourdough.
4 Serve tomato mixture, sliced meats, pâté and toasts with mushrooms and salad.

PICKLED MUSHROOMS
Heat oil in large frying pan, add mushrooms, chillies and thyme; stir over medium heat 1 minute. Stir in sugar then vinegar; stir until mushrooms are tender. Cool, season to taste.

CARROT AND TURMERIC SALAD
Combine ingredients in medium bowl; season to taste.

A charcuterie plate consists of cured or prepared meats (most often pork). To save time, purchase various preserves and dips from the supermarket instead of making the pickled mushrooms and carrot salad. Water crackers and oat cakes can be served instead of the sourdough.

Christmas Dinner

SMOKED TROUT SALAD
with Salsa Verde Dressing

PREP + COOK TIME 45 MINUTES SERVES 6

500g (1 pound) kipfler (fingerling) potatoes
125g (4 ounces) green beans
3 cups (350g) firmly packed trimmed watercress
1 green oak leaf lettuce, leaves separated
300g (9½ ounces) hot-smoked trout, skinned, flaked

SALSA VERDE DRESSING
1 slice (50g) white bread, torn coarsely
1½ tablespoons red wine vinegar
¼ cup each loosely packed fresh basil leaves, flat-leaf parsley leaves and mint leaves
2 drained anchovy fillets, chopped coarsely
1 clove garlic, chopped coarsely
2 teaspoons rinsed, drained capers
2 tablespoons olive oil

1. Boil, steam or microwave potatoes and beans, separately, until tender; drain. Rinse under cold water; drain. Halve potatoes lengthways.
2. Meanwhile, make salsa verde dressing.
3. Combine potatoes, beans and two-thirds of the dressing in large bowl. Place watercress and lettuce on serving platter. Top with potato mixture and trout; drizzle with remaining dressing.

SALSA VERDE DRESSING
Combine bread and vinegar in small bowl; stand about 5 minutes or until vinegar is almost absorbed. Blend or process herbs, anchovy, garlic, capers and bread mixture to a coarse paste. Stir in oil. Season to taste.

PROSCIUTTO-WRAPPED PRAWNS
with Bean Salad

PREP + COOK TIME 50 MINUTES   SERVES 6

24 uncooked medium king prawns (shrimp)(1kg)
4 slices prosciutto (60g)
150g (5 ounces) green beans, trimmed
150g (5 ounces) yellow beans, trimmed
340g (11 ounces) asparagus, trimmed
1 tablespoon olive oil
⅓ cup (100g) aïoli
2 tablespoons water
500g (1 pound) rocket (arugula), trimmed
⅓ cup (50g) finely chopped drained sun-dried tomatoes in oil

1 Shell and devein prawns, leaving tails intact.
2 Cut each slice of prosciutto in half crossways and then into thirds lengthways. Wrap a strip of prosciutto around each prawn.
3 Boil, steam or microwave beans and asparagus, separately, until tender; drain. Rinse under cold water, drain.
4 Heat oil in large frying pan; cook prawns until browned and just cooked through.
5 Meanwhile, combine aïoli and the water in a small bowl.
6 Place rocket, beans and asparagus on serving platter or plates. Top with prawns and tomato; drizzle with aïoli mixture.

Aïoli is a garlic mayonnaise; it is available from supermarkets in the refrigerated section. You need to buy two bunches of rocket for this recipe.

PRAWN COCKTAIL WITH ZUCCHINI
and Mint Salad

PREP TIME 25 MINUTES (+ STANDING)   SERVES 6

⅓ cup (80ml) lemon juice
1 tablespoon red wine vinegar
2 tablespoons olive oil
2 small zucchini (180g), cut into ribbons
3 radishes (110g), trimmed, sliced thinly
1 baby cos (romaine) lettuce (180g), leaves torn
½ cup loosely packed fresh mint leaves
1 large avocado (320g), cut into small wedges
18 cooked medium king prawns (shrimp) (800g), shelled, deveined

1 Combine juice, vinegar and oil in medium bowl, add zucchini; turn to coat in dressing. Stand zucchini mixture 20 minutes. Add radish, lettuce and mint; toss gently to combine. Season to taste.
2 Divide zucchini salad and avocado into six serving glasses; top with prawns, drizzle with any remaining dressing.

Cut the zucchini into ribbons using a vegetable peeler, V-slicer or mandoline.

(PHOTOGRAPH PAGE 144)

PRAWN COCKTAIL WITH
Zucchini and Mint Salad
(RECIPE PAGE 143)

QUAIL SALAD WITH
Pomegranate Dressing
(RECIPE PAGE 146)

QUAIL SALAD WITH *Pomegranate Dressing*

PREP + COOK TIME 45 MINUTES   SERVES 6

4 quails (640g)
2 tablespoons pomegranate molasses
2 tablespoons honey
1 tablespoon wholegrain mustard
¼ cup (60ml) olive oil
2 tablespoons lemon juice
½ cup (60g) coarsely chopped pecans
2 medium radicchio (400g), leaves torn
100g (3 ounces) baby spinach leaves

1. Rinse quails under cold water; pat dry with absorbent paper. Using kitchen scissors, discard necks from quails. Cut along each side of quail's backbone; discard backbones. Halve each quail along breastbone; cut each half into two pieces.
2. Preheat oven to 200°C/400°F. Line oven tray with baking paper.
3. Combine molasses, honey, mustard and 2 tablespoons of the oil in medium bowl. Transfer one-third of the molasses mixture into a jug; stir in juice. Reserve for dressing.
4. Add quail to remaining molasses mixture, turn to coat. Heat remaining oil in large frying pan; cook quail about 2 minutes each side or until browned. Transfer to oven tray. Roast, uncovered, about 10 minutes or until cooked through, adding nuts to tray for last 5 minutes of cooking time.
5. Place radicchio and spinach on serving plates. Top with quail and nuts; drizzle with reserved dressing.

(PHOTOGRAPH PAGE 145)

BARBECUED *Ham*

PREP + COOK TIME 2 HOURS (+ STANDING)   SERVES 16

7kg (14-pound) cooked leg of ham
2 tablespoons dijon mustard
⅔ cup (150g) firmly packed light brown sugar
½ cup (125ml) pineapple juice
½ cup (125ml) sweet sherry
¼ cup (55g) firmly packed light brown sugar, extra
2 cloves garlic, halved lengthways
¼ teaspoon ground cloves
1 medium pineapple (1.2kg), halved, sliced thickly

1. Cut through rind of ham 10cm (4 inches) from shank end of the leg. To remove rind, run thumb around edge of rind just under skin. Start pulling rind from widest edge of ham; continue to pull rind carefully away from the fat up to the shank end. Remove rind completely. Score across the fat at about 4cm (1½-inch) intervals, cutting lightly through the surface of the fat (not the meat) in a diamond pattern.
2. Place ham in disposable aluminium baking dish; rub ham with combined mustard and sugar. Place on heated barbecue; cook, covered, using indirect method, following manufacturer's instructions, for 1 hour.
3. Meanwhile, stir juice, sherry, extra sugar, garlic and clove in small saucepan over heat until sugar dissolves. Simmer, uncovered, about 10 minutes or until glaze reduces by half. Brush ham with glaze; cook, covered, using indirect method a further 45 minutes, brushing several times with glaze during cooking. Remove from barbecue, cover ham loosely with foil; stand 15 minutes before slicing.
4. Meanwhile, cook pineapple on heated barbecue, brushing with remaining glaze during cooking.
5. Serve ham with pineapple.

BARBECUED
Ham

HERBED SALMON WITH CAPERS
and Fennel Remoulade

PREP + COOK TIME 40 MINUTES SERVES 8

1.5kg (3-pound) piece salmon fillet, skin on
2 tablespoons olive oil
½ cup each coarsely chopped fresh flat-leaf parsley and mint
1 clove garlic, crushed
2 teaspoons finely grated lemon rind
2 tablespoons coarsely chopped rinsed, drained capers
1 fresh long red chilli, sliced thinly

FENNEL REMOULADE
1 tablespoon dijon mustard
½ cup (150g) mayonnaise
2 tablespoons lemon juice
1 tablespoon finely chopped fresh tarragon
2 medium fennel bulbs (600g), shaved

1 Preheat oven to 200°C/400°F.
2 Place salmon in large baking dish lined with baking paper. Brush with half the oil; season. Bake, uncovered, about 15 minutes or until cooked as desired.
3 Meanwhile, make fennel remoulade.
4 Combine herbs, garlic, rind, capers and chilli in medium bowl.
5 Transfer salmon to serving platter. Sprinkle with herb mixture, drizzle with remaining oil. Serve with remoulade, and lemon wedges if you like.

FENNEL REMOULADE
Combine ingredients in medium bowl; season to taste.

STEAMED FISH WITH GINGER
and Green Onion Salad

PREP + COOK TIME 40 MINUTES SERVES 6

6 green onions (scallions), sliced thinly
8cm (3¼-inch) piece fresh ginger (40g), shredded finely
1.5kg (3-pound) cleaned whole fish
½ cup (125ml) chicken stock
2 tablespoons chinese cooking wine
1½ tablespoons light soy sauce
2 teaspoons white (granulated) sugar
1 tablespoon peanut oil
1 cup lightly packed fresh coriander (cilantro) sprigs
1 teaspoon sesame oil

1 Combine onion and ginger in small bowl. Pat fish dry with absorbent paper. Use sharp knife to score fish in a criss-cross pattern on both sides. Place one-third of the ginger mixture in fish cavity.
2 Bring large wok of water to the boil. Line large steamer basket (large enough to fit neatly over the wok) with a heatproof plate or shallow dish lined with baking paper.
3 Spread one-third of the remaining ginger mixture over baking paper; top with fish, sprinkle with half the remaining ginger mixture. Place steamer basket over simmering water. Pour combined stock, wine, sauce and half the sugar over the fish. Cover; steam fish about 15 minutes or until cooked through. Transfer fish to serving platter; pour hot stock mixture over fish. Sprinkle with remaining ginger mixture and remaining sugar.
4 Heat peanut oil in small saucepan until very hot; pour over fish. Sprinkle fish with coriander; drizzle with sesame oil.

SERVING SUGGESTION
Serve with steamed rice, buk choy or gai lan (chinese broccoli).

We used coral trout. If it is unavailable, use snapper, bream, barramundi or silver perch. We used a large bamboo steamer for this recipe; a rack fitted snugly into the wok or a fish poacher would work just as well.

Christmas is one of those special occasions in the year when you can spoil your family with the luxury of lobster. Purchased cooked lobster (from your fishmonger) coupled with a simple dressed salad of fennel and endive, makes this dish very easy and quick to make.

LOBSTER WITH
Fennel Salad

PREP TIME 35 MINUTES (+ STANDING) SERVES 6

1 medium fennel bulb (300g)
150g (5 ounces) curly endive
3 cooked lobsters (1.8kg), halved lengthways

GREEN OLIVE AND CURRANT SALSA
3 medium lemons (420g)
⅓ cup (70g) seeded small green olives, chopped coarsely
2 tablespoons rinsed, drained baby capers
2 tablespoons dried currants
⅓ cup finely chopped fresh flat-leaf parsley
2 tablespoons olive oil

1. Make green olive and currant salsa.
2. Reserve fronds from fennel. Slice fennel thinly with V-slicer or mandoline. Combine fennel and endive in medium bowl, sprinkle with half the salsa.
3. Divide lobster and salad among serving plates. Drizzle with remaining salsa; sprinkle with reserved fennel fronds.

GREEN OLIVE AND CURRANT SALSA
Finely grate rind from one lemon. Peel rind thickly from all lemons to remove white pith. Segment lemons over medium bowl to catch juice. Chop lemon flesh finely; add to bowl with rind and remaining ingredients. Stand 20 minutes; season to taste.

PORK HOCK WITH PEANUT CARAMEL
and Pickled Cucumber
(RECIPE PAGES 156 & 157)

PORK HOCK WITH PEANUT CARAMEL
and Pickled Cucumber

PREP + COOK TIME 3 HOURS (REFRIGERATION) SERVES 4

4 cloves garlic, crushed
4cm (1½-inch) piece fresh ginger (20g), grated
2 fresh small red thai (serrano) chillies, chopped finely
½ cup (125ml) fish sauce
2 pork hocks (2kg)
1.5 litres (6 cups) chicken stock
2 cups (500ml) water
3cm (1¼-inch) piece fresh ginger (15g), shredded finely
10 white peppercorns, crushed
2 tablespoons kecap manis
1 tablespoon grated palm sugar
2 star anise
1 cinnamon stick
¼ cup (60ml) peanut oil

PEANUT CARAMEL
1 cup (270g) grated palm sugar
2 tablespoons fish sauce
4cm (1½-inch) piece fresh ginger (20g), shredded finely
1 fresh small red thai (serrano) chilli, sliced thinly
1 star anise
1 cinnamon stick
½ cup (70g) roasted unsalted peanuts, chopped coarsely

PICKLED CUCUMBER
2 tablespoons rice wine vinegar
1 teaspoon grated palm sugar
1 teaspoon fish sauce
2 lebanese cucumbers (260g), seeded, sliced thinly
2 fresh long red chillies, sliced thinly
½ cup loosely packed fresh coriander (cilantro) leaves

1. Combine garlic, grated ginger, chilli and 2 tablespoons of the fish sauce in small bowl. Score skin of pork two or three times on each side. Using gloves, rub chilli paste into pork. Place pork in a dish; cover, refrigerate overnight.
2. Preheat oven to 150°C/300°F.
3. Bring stock, the water, shredded ginger, peppercorns, kecap manis, sugar, star anise, cinnamon and remaining fish sauce to the boil in large flameproof dish. Add pork to dish; cover, cook in oven about 2½ hours or until pork is tender, turning halfway through cooking. Remove pork from liquid; reserve ⅓ cup liquid for the peanut caramel, discard remaining liquid.
4. Meanwhile, make peanut caramel and pickled cucumber.
5. Heat oil in large frying pan; cook pork until browned all over. Transfer to serving platter. Drizzle with peanut caramel; top with pickled cucumber.

PEANUT CARAMEL
Stir sugar and half the fish sauce in medium saucepan over heat until sugar is dissolved; bring to the boil. Reduce heat; simmer, uncovered, without stirring, about 5 minutes or until caramelised. Add ginger, chilli, star anise, cinnamon and reserved liquid; simmer, uncovered, about 5 minutes or until syrupy. Add remaining fish sauce and peanuts.

PICKLED CUCUMBER
Stir vinegar, sugar and sauce in small saucepan over heat until sugar is dissolved. Pour over combined cucumber and chilli in small bowl; cool. Just before serving, stir in coriander.

SERVING SUGGESTION
Serve with steamed jasmine rice and lime wedges.

(PHOTOGRAPH PAGE 155)

GOD REST YE MERRY *Gentlemen*

EMBELLISH a classic Christmas wreath with a centre of candles for a spectacular **TABLE SETTING**.
YOU WILL NEED a wreath (they can be ordered from your local flower shop to any design you like), seven clean small jars and seven **WHITE CANDLES**.
TO MAKE SURE THE CANDLE is secure in the jar, place the jar on a worktop, hold the flat end of your candle over the jar and using a taper, melt a few drops of wax into the base of the jar.
IMMEDIATELY PRESS the hot end of your candle into the melted wax, hold in place for a second or two until set.
PLACE THE WREATH on the table and arrange the candles in their jars in the **CENTRE OF THE WREATH**.
Light the candles just prior to *guests arriving*.

BARBECUED DUCK
with Caramelised Fennel Oranges

PREP + COOK TIME 40 MINUTES SERVES 6

6 duck breast fillets (900g)
2 small fennel bulbs (400g)
1 small radicchio (150g)
1 tablespoon olive oil
1 tablespoon red wine vinegar

CARAMELISED FENNEL ORANGES
5 medium oranges (1.2kg)
⅓ cup (75g) firmly packed light brown sugar
1 teaspoon fennel seeds
1 tablespoon water
½ cup (125ml) orange-flavoured liqueur
2 tablespoons red wine vinegar

1. Make caramelised fennel oranges.
2. Season duck. Cook duck, skin-side down, on heated grill plate (or grill or barbecue) over high heat about 5 minutes or until skin is crisp. Turn duck, cook a further 5 minutes or until duck is almost cooked through. Transfer to plate; cover, stand 5 minutes.
3. Reserve fennel fronds. Slice fennel finely on V-slicer or mandoline. Combine fennel, fronds and radicchio leaves in medium bowl. Drizzle with 2 tablespoons orange syrup from caramelised fennel oranges then combined oil and vinegar; season to taste.
4. Serve duck and fennel salad with warm caramelised fennel oranges.

CARAMELISED FENNEL ORANGES
Peel and thickly slice three of the oranges; place in heatproof bowl. Remove the rind from one of the remaining oranges with a zester. Squeeze the remaining oranges; you will need ½ cup juice. Stir sugar, seeds and the water in small saucepan, without boiling, until sugar is dissolved. Bring to the boil; boil, uncovered, without stirring, until syrup starts to caramelise. Add rind, juice and liqueur to pan. Reduce heat, simmer, uncovered, about 5 minutes or until rind softens; remove from heat. Add vinegar; pour over oranges in bowl. Cool 10 minutes.

BOURBON-GLAZED HAM
with Warm Potato and Celery Salad

PREP + COOK TIME 1 HOUR 35 MINUTES (+ STANDING) SERVES 16

7kg (14-pound) cooked leg of ham
whole cloves, to decorate
1 cup (220g) firmly packed light brown sugar
¼ cup (60ml) bourbon
1 cup (250ml) water

WARM POTATO AND CELERY SALAD
1kg (2 pounds) kipfler (fingerling) potatoes, peeled
1 tablespoon wholegrain mustard
2 tablespoons sherry vinegar
¼ cup extra virgin olive oil
3 stalks celery (450g), trimmed, sliced thinly
1 small red onion (100g), sliced thinly
½ cup coarsely chopped fresh flat-leaf parsley
¼ cup (40g) seeded kalamata olives, drained

1. Preheat oven to 180°C/350°F.
2. Cut through rind of ham 10cm (4 inches) from shank end of the leg. To remove rind, run thumb around edge of rind just under skin. Start pulling rind from widest edge of ham; continue to pull rind carefully away from the fat up to the shank end. Remove rind completely. Score across the fat at about 4cm (1½-inch) intervals, cutting lightly through the surface of the fat (not the meat) in a diamond pattern. Decorate with cloves.
3. Combine sugar and bourbon in small bowl.
4. Pour the water into large baking dish; place ham on oiled wire rack in dish. Brush ham all over with one-third of the bourbon glaze. Roast, uncovered, 1¼ hours or until browned, brushing often with remaining glaze. Cover ham loosely with foil; stand 15 minutes before slicing.
5. Meanwhile, make warm potato and celery salad.
6. Serve ham with salad.

WARM POTATO AND CELERY SALAD
Boil, steam or microwave potatoes until tender; drain. Meanwhile, whisk mustard and vinegar in small bowl, season; whisk in oil. When potatoes are cool enough to handle, slice thickly. Combine potato in serving bowl with half the dressing. Add celery, onion, parsley, olives and remaining dressing; toss gently to combine. Sprinkle with some celery leaves, if you like.

Reserve the rind from the ham and use it to cover the cut surface. This will keep the ham moist during storage. You can also freeze the ham and the ham bone. Cut the meat from the bone and wrap separately in plastic wrap. Place in airtight containers. Label, date and freeze for up to one month. Thaw in the fridge overnight. This simple glaze also works well with brandy or whiskey.

Christmas Dinner

BARBECUED FILLET OF BEEF
with Caramelised Radish and Onion

PREP + COOK TIME 1 HOUR 10 MINUTES (+ REFRIGERATION & STANDING) **SERVES 6**

1.5kg (3-pound) beef eye fillet
1 cup (250ml) dry red wine
4 cloves garlic, sliced thinly
4 fresh thyme sprigs
4 fresh bay leaves
½ teaspoon cracked black peppercorns
1 tablespoon olive oil
60g (2 ounces) trimmed watercress

CARAMELISED RADISH AND ONION
¼ cup (55g) caster (superfine) sugar
¼ cup (60ml) white wine vinegar
1 medium red onion (170g), cut into thin wedges
6 radishes (240g), cut into wedges
4 cloves garlic, sliced thinly

1. Trim fillet of any fat and membrane. Tuck thin end of fillet underneath. Using kitchen string, tie beef firmly at 2cm (¾-inch) intervals to keep shape. Combine wine, garlic, thyme, bay leaves and peppercorns in dish; add beef, turn to coat in marinade. Cover, refrigerate overnight, turning three times.
2. Remove beef from marinade; discard marinade. Pat beef dry with absorbent paper; brush with oil, then season.
3. Cook beef on heated barbecue until browned all over. Cover with lid or foil; cook about 45 minutes for medium or until done as desired. Transfer beef to heated plate; cover with foil, stand 20 minutes.
4. Meanwhile, make caramelised radish and onion.
5. Serve sliced beef with caramelised radish and onion and watercress.

CARAMELISED RADISH AND ONION
Heat medium frying pan; add sugar to pan. Cook over medium heat until sugar turns golden brown. Add vinegar carefully, sugar will bubble fiercely; stir until sugar dissolves. Bring to the boil; simmer, uncovered, until syrupy. Stir in onion, radish and garlic; simmer about 5 minutes or until onion softens.

GINGER MARMALADE
Glazed Ham

PREP + COOK TIME 1 HOUR 45 MINUTES **SERVES** 12

365g (12 ounces) ginger marmalade
⅓ cup (80ml) maple syrup
½ cup (110g) firmly packed light brown sugar
1 cup (250ml) dry ginger ale
7kg (15-pound) cooked leg of ham
2 tablespoons cloves

1. Bring marmalade, syrup, sugar and ginger ale to the boil in small saucepan. Reduce heat to medium; simmer, uncovered, about 10 minutes or until reduced by half.
2. Meanwhile, place oven shelf in lowest position. Preheat oven to 180°C/350°F.
3. Using a sharp knife, cut a zigzag pattern through ham rind about 12cm (5 inches) from the shank end of leg. Remove rind from ham by sliding your hand between the rind and the fat layer. Discard rind. Score fat diagonally at 2cm (¾-inch) intervals to form a diamond pattern. Stud centre of diamonds with cloves.
4. Place ham on wire rack placed in large baking dish. Wrap shank in foil. Brush ham with half the marmalade mixture. Bake ham, basting with remaining marmalade mixture, about 1¼ hours or until glaze is browned lightly. Serve warm or cold.

If the ham doesn't fit into your oven, or if your oven is full, bake the ham in a covered barbecue, using indirect heat, and following the manufacturer's instructions.
Store cold leftover ham in a calico ham bag. Ham bags can be purchased from kitchenware stores and major supermarkets.
If refrigerator space is a problem, remove meat from the bone and refrigerate, covered in plastic wrap for up to 10 days.

ITALIAN-STYLE TURKEY ROLL WITH
Pork and Fennel Sausage Stuffing

PREP + COOK TIME 1 HOUR 30 MINUTES **SERVES** 12

1.5kg (3-pound) single turkey breast, skin on
1 tablespoon olive oil
6 baby fennel bulbs (780g), halved
1 medium lemon (140g), quartered
½ cup (125ml) dry white wine

PORK AND FENNEL SAUSAGE STUFFING
½ cup (35g) stale breadcrumbs
⅓ cup (80ml) milk
1 tablespoon olive oil
1 medium brown onion (150g), chopped finely
2 cloves garlic, crushed
70g (2½ ounces) rocket (arugula), chopped finely
7 pork and fennel sausages (560g), cases removed

1. Preheat oven to 200°C/400°F.
2. Make pork and fennel sausage stuffing.
3. Pat turkey dry with absorbent paper; place skin-side down on board. Starting from one long edge, slice through centre, horizontally, not quite through to other side, to open out flat. Spread with stuffing. Roll turkey tightly to secure stuffing. Using kitchen string, tie into a neat roll at 2.5cm (1-inch) intervals.
4. Heat oil in large baking dish in oven 5 minutes. Add turkey roll; turn to coat. Place fennel and lemon around turkey; add wine to dish. Roast, uncovered, about 50 minutes or until turkey is cooked through, basting turkey frequently.
5. Cover turkey loosely with foil; stand 10 minutes before slicing. Serve with fennel and lemon.

PORK AND FENNEL SAUSAGE STUFFING
Combine breadcrumbs and milk in small bowl. Heat oil in medium frying pan; cook onion, stirring occasionally, until tender. Stir in garlic, then stir in rocket until wilted. Transfer to medium bowl; cool 20 minutes. Stir in sausage mince and breadcrumb mixture; season.

It's important not to overcrowd the turkey, fennel and lemon in the baking dish so they cook evenly and caramelise.
When the roll is cooked, juices should run clear when tested with a skewer.

ROLLED LAMB SHOULDER WITH HARISSA
and Couscous Stuffing

PREP + COOK TIME *1 HOUR 30 MINUTES* **SERVES** *8*

⅓ cup (65g) couscous
⅓ cup (80ml) boiling water
2 x 750g (3 pounds) boned lamb shoulders
¼ cup (40g) pine nuts, roasted
½ cup coarsely chopped fresh mint
1 tablespoon olive oil

HARISSA
2 medium red capsicum (bell peppers) (400g)
1 tablespoon olive oil
1 small red onion (100g), chopped coarsely
4 cloves garlic, chopped coarsely
1 tablespoon ground coriander
1 tablespoon caraway seeds
2 teaspoons ground cumin
1 fresh red thai (serrano) chilli, chopped coarsely
1 tablespoon finely chopped preserved lemon
1 teaspoon dried mint

1. Preheat oven to 200°C/400°F.
2. Make harissa.
3. Combine couscous with the water in medium bowl; stand 5 minutes. Stir harissa into couscous.
4. Place lamb, fat-side down, on board. Spread couscous mixture over lamb; top with pine nuts and mint. Roll tightly to enclose filling; secure with kitchen string at 2cm (¾-inch) intervals.
5. Heat oil in large baking dish; add lamb, cook until browned all over.
6. Transfer dish to oven; roast, uncovered, about 45 minutes. Cover lamb with foil; stand 10 minutes before serving.

HARISSA
Place capsicum on oven tray; roast about 20 minutes or until skin blisters and blackens (leave the oven on). Cover capsicum with plastic wrap, stand for 5 minutes; peel away skin, discard stems and seeds. Meanwhile, heat oil in small frying pan; cook onion and garlic, stirring, until softened. Add spices; cook, stirring, until fragrant. Process capsicum and onion mixture with remaining ingredients until smooth.

SERVING SUGGESTION
Serve with grilled flat bread and rocket (arugula); accompany with greek yogurt.

You could use 2 tablespoons finely chopped fresh mint instead of dried mint when making the harissa.

BUTTERFLIED LAMB
with Fresh Mint Sauce

PREP + COOK TIME 40 MINUTES (+ REFRIGERATION & STANDING) **SERVES** 10

½ cup (90g) honey
1 tablespoon wholegrain mustard
2kg (4-pound) butterflied leg of lamb
¼ cup loosely packed fresh rosemary sprigs

MINT SAUCE
½ cup (110g) firmly packed light brown sugar
½ cup (125ml) water
1½ cups (375ml) cider vinegar
½ cup finely chopped fresh mint

1. Make mint sauce.
2. Combine a quarter of the mint sauce, honey and mustard in large shallow dish; add lamb, turn to coat in marinade. Cover; refrigerate 3 hours or overnight, turning occasionally. Refrigerate remaining mint sauce, separately.
3. Drain lamb; place, fat-side down, on heated oiled grill plate (or grill or barbecue). Cover lamb loosely with foil; cook about 10 minutes or until browned underneath. Uncover; turn lamb, sprinkle with rosemary. Cook, covered, about 10 minutes or until cooked as desired (or cook by indirect heat in covered barbecue following manufacturer's instructions). Remove from heat; stand, covered, 15 minutes.
4. Slice lamb thinly; serve with remaining mint sauce.

MINT SAUCE
Stir sugar and the water in small saucepan over heat, without boiling, until sugar dissolves. Bring to the boil. Reduce heat; simmer, uncovered, without stirring, 5 minutes or until syrup thickens slightly. Combine syrup, vinegar and mint in small bowl.

SERVING SUGGESTION
Serve with baby potatoes and a tomato and radish salad.

The mint sauce can be made several days ahead. Ask the butcher to butterfly a leg of lamb for you.

PEPPER-CRUSTED BEEF WITH MUSTARD
and Crème Fraîche Sauce

PREP + COOK TIME 1 HOUR 15 MINUTES SERVES 8

2 tablespoons mixed dried peppercorns
2 teaspoons sea salt flakes
2 tablespoons olive oil
1.5kg (3-pound) piece beef eye fillet
MUSTARD AND CREME FRAICHE SAUCE
1 tablespoon olive oil
1 tablespoon plain (all-purpose) flour
½ cup (125ml) dry white wine
1 tablespoon wholegrain mustard
1 tablespoon dijon mustard
1¼ cups (310ml) pouring cream
¼ cup (60g) crème fraîche
2 tablespoons lemon juice

1. Preheat oven to 200°C/400°F.
2. Using a mortar and pestle, crush peppercorns; combine in small bowl with salt.
3. Rub half the oil over beef; sprinkle with peppercorn mixture, press on lightly.
4. Heat remaining oil in large flameproof dish; cook beef until browned all over. Transfer dish to oven; roast beef, uncovered, about 45 minutes or until cooked as desired. Stand beef, covered with foil, 10 minutes.
5. Meanwhile, make mustard and crème fraîche sauce.
6. Serve sliced beef with sauce.

MUSTARD AND CREME FRAICHE SAUCE
Heat oil in medium frying pan, add flour; cook, stirring, until mixture bubbles and browns lightly. Gradually stir in wine; bring to the boil, stirring. Reduce heat; simmer, uncovered, until liquid reduces by half. Stir in mustards and cream; simmer, stirring, about 5 minutes or until sauce thickens. Remove from heat, stir in crème fraîche and juice; season to taste.

SERVING SUGGESTION
Serve with steamed carrots, asparagus and green beans.

It is fine to use just one 300ml carton of cream for this recipe.

PORK LOIN WITH
Spiced Orange Relish

PREP + COOK TIME 1 HOUR 30 MINUTES SERVES 6

1.5kg (3-pound) rolled loin of pork
2 tablespoons olive oil
1 tablespoon coarse cooking salt (kosher salt)
500g (1 pound) spinach, trimmed, shredded finely
½ cup (70g) slivered almonds, roasted
200g (6½ ounces) fetta cheese, crumbled
1 tablespoon red wine vinegar

SPICED ORANGE RELISH
3 medium oranges (720g)
1 cup (220g) white (granulated) sugar
1 cup (250ml) water
⅓ cup (80ml) cider vinegar
¾ teaspoon fennel seeds
5 cardamom pods, bruised
4 cloves
1 cinnamon stick

1. Make spiced orange relish.
2. Meanwhile, preheat oven to 220°C/425°F.
3. Pat pork dry with absorbent paper. Rub pork with half the oil, then salt; place in large shallow baking dish, seam-side down. Roast, uncovered, about 40 minutes or until rind crackles.
4. Reduce oven to 200°C/400°F; roast pork, uncovered, about 30 minutes or until cooked. Cover pork loosely with foil; stand pork 10 minutes before slicing thinly.
5. Meanwhile, combine spinach, nuts, cheese, vinegar and remaining oil in large bowl; season to taste.
6. Serve sliced pork with salad and relish; drizzle with pan juices.

SPICED ORANGE RELISH
Quarter unpeeled oranges; slice quarters thinly, discard seeds. Stir sugar, the water, vinegar and spices in medium heavy-based saucepan over heat until sugar dissolves. Bring to the boil; stir in orange. Reduce heat; simmer, stirring occasionally, about 1 hour or until rind is tender and relish has thickened. Cool.

The relish can be made up to three weeks ahead; keep, covered, in the refrigerator until ready to use. Return the relish to room temperature before serving. This recipe makes about 1½ cups of relish – more than you need.

CHICKPEA AND CHILLI
Walnut Salad

PREP TIME 20 MINUTES SERVES 8

800g (1½ pounds) canned chickpeas (garbanzo beans), drained, rinsed
1 cup each coarsely chopped fresh flat-leaf parsley and mint
1 cup (160g) seeded green olives, chopped coarsely
4 green onions (scallions), sliced thinly
2 fresh long green chillies, sliced thinly
1 medium red capsicum (bell pepper) (200g), chopped finely
1 cup (100g) roasted walnuts, chopped coarsely

DRESSING
¼ cup (60ml) olive oil
¼ cup (60ml) lemon juice

1 Make dressing.
2 Combine salad ingredients in large bowl.
3 Just before serving, drizzle dressing over salad; toss gently to combine.

DRESSING
Place ingredients in screw-top jar; shake well. Season to taste.

Prepare the dressing and assemble the salad on Christmas morning. Dress the salad just before serving. This is a great salad to take on a picnic; pack the dressing and salad in separate containers and assemble on location.

BEAN SALAD
with Basil Dressing

PREP TIME 15 MINUTES **SERVES** 4

400g (12½ ounces) canned butter beans, drained, rinsed
400g (12½ ounces) canned borlotti beans, drained, rinsed
250g (8 ounces) cherry tomatoes, quartered
12 cherry bocconcini cheese (180g), halved
60g (2 ounces) baby rocket (arugula) leaves
½ cup (80g) roasted pine nuts

BASIL DRESSING
2 tablespoons olive oil
2 tablespoons white wine vinegar
2 teaspoons white balsamic vinegar
2 tablespoons coarsely chopped fresh basil
¼ cup (60ml) pouring cream

1. Make basil dressing.
2. Combine salad ingredients in large bowl.
3. Just before serving, drizzle dressing over salad; toss gently to combine.

BASIL DRESSING
Whisk oil, vinegars and basil in small bowl; whisk in cream. Season to taste.

Prepare the dressing and assemble the salad on Christmas morning. Dress the salad just before serving.

FRESH CHERRY AND
Pistachio Tabbouleh

PREP TIME 30 MINUTES (+ STANDING) **SERVES** 8

1½ cups (240g) burghul
2 cups (500ml) boiling water
500g (1 pound) fresh cherries, seeded, halved
1 cup (140g) pistachios, chopped coarsely
2 cups firmly packed fresh mint leaves, chopped finely
1 cup firmly packed fresh flat-leaf parsley leaves, chopped finely
1 small red onion (100g), chopped finely
½ cup each loosely packed small mint and flat-leaf parsley leaves, extra

RED WINE VINEGAR DRESSING
½ cup (125ml) olive oil
⅓ cup (80ml) red wine vinegar

1 Combine burghul and the water in large heatproof bowl. Stand about 15 minutes or until burghul is tender and the water absorbed.
2 Meanwhile, make red wine vinegar dressing.
3 Add cherries, nuts, chopped herbs and onion to burghul. Stir in dressing; season to taste.
4 Serve tabbouleh sprinkled with extra herbs.

RED WINE VINEGAR DRESSING
Whisk ingredients in small bowl; season to taste.

You need about three bunches of mint for this recipe.

GREEN PAPAYA *Salad*

PREP TIME 45 MINUTES (+ STANDING) SERVES 8

3 limes
1 medium green papaya (1kg)
16 snake beans (225g), sliced diagonally
500g (1 pound) cherry tomatoes, quartered
1 cup each loosely packed thai basil leaves and fresh coriander (cilantro) leaves
½ cup (70g) unsalted roasted peanuts, chopped coarsely

PEANUT AND GARLIC DRESSING
2 tablespoons dried shrimp
6 cloves garlic
1 teaspoon salt
¼ cup (35g) unsalted roasted peanuts, chopped coarsely
2 fresh small red thai (serrano) chillies, chopped
⅔ cup (180g) grated palm sugar
¼ cup (60ml) fish sauce

1. Peel limes, removing white pith. Segment limes over bowl to catch juice; reserve juice for dressing.
2. Make peanut and garlic dressing.
3. Peel papaya, quarter lengthways, discard seeds; cut papaya into long thin strips.
4. Place papaya, beans and tomato in large bowl with dressing; toss gently to combine. Stand 20 minutes.
5. Add herbs and peanuts to papaya mixture; toss gently to combine.

PEANUT AND GARLIC DRESSING
Place shrimp in heatproof bowl; cover with boiling water. Stand about 10 minutes or until shrimp are soft. Using mortar and pestle, grind garlic and salt until smooth. Add peanuts and drained shrimp; pound to smooth paste. Add chilli; pound until crushed coarsely. Stir in sugar, sauce and reserved lime juice.

Add more or less chilli, sugar and lime juice to suit your taste.

CHERRY WALNUT
and Fetta Salad

CHERRY, WALNUT
and Fetta Salad

PREP TIME 20 MINUTES **SERVES** 8

125g (4 ounces) mesclun
¼ cup coarsely chopped fresh chives
1 cup (125g) seeded fresh cherries, halved
½ cup (50g) walnuts, roasted
100g (3 ounces) fetta cheese, crumbled

LEMON DRESSING
2 teaspoons finely grated lemon rind
2 tablespoons tarragon vinegar
1 tablespoon lemon juice
1 teaspoon dijon mustard
¼ cup (60ml) olive oil

1. Make lemon dressing.
2. Place mesclun, chives, cherries, half the nuts and half the cheese in large bowl with dressing; toss gently to combine.
3. Serve salad sprinkled with remaining nuts and remaining cheese.

LEMON DRESSING
Whisk ingredients in small bowl until combined; season to taste.

When cherries aren't in season, make this salad using quartered canned baby beetroot (beets), instead.

PEA, MINT
and Almond Salad

PREP + COOK TIME 30 MINUTES **SERVES** 6

150g (5 ounces) snow peas, trimmed
150g (5 ounces) sugar snap peas, trimmed
125g (4 ounces) snow pea sprouts, trimmed
150g (5 ounces) young pea tendrils, trimmed
1 cup loosely packed fresh mint leaves
½ cup (70g) slivered almonds, roasted

MUSTARD AND CIDER DRESSING
2 tablespoons olive oil
1 tablespoon cider vinegar
2 teaspoons wholegrain mustard

1. Cook snow peas and sugar snap peas in boiling salted water about 2 minutes or until barely tender; drain. Rinse under cold running water; drain.
2. Make mustard and cider dressing.
3. Place peas in large bowl with sprouts, tendrils, mint, nuts and dressing; toss gently to combine.

MUSTARD AND CIDER DRESSING
Combine ingredients in small bowl; season to taste.

Snow pea sprouts and pea tendrils can be hard to get sometimes – use bean sprouts or any other type of sprouts instead.

(PHOTOGRAPH PAGE 188)

PEA, MINT
and Almond Salad
(RECIPE PAGE 187)

PEACH, PROSCIUTTO
and Mozzarella Salad
(RECIPE PAGE 190)

PEACH, PROSCIUTTO *and Mozzarella Salad*

PREP TIME *15 MINUTES* **SERVES 8**

4 medium yellow peaches (600g), cut into wedges
16 slices prosciutto (240g)
3 buffalo mozzarella (390g), torn
⅓ cup firmly packed fresh flat-leaf parsley leaves
¼ cup firmly packed fresh mint leaves
2 tablespoons olive oil
1 tablespoon balsamic vinegar

1. Place peach, prosciutto and cheese on plates, sprinkle with herbs.
2. Combine oil and vinegar in small bowl; season. Drizzle dressing over salad.

This simple salad will be all the better for using a good quality aged balsamic vinegar in the dressing. The flavour will be more intense and the consistency more syrupy than those of younger balsamic vinegars.

(PHOTOGRAPH PAGE 189)

WARM KIPFLER AND CUCUMBER SALAD *with Dill*

PREP + COOK TIME *30 MINUTES* **SERVES 6**

1 medium red onion (170g), sliced thinly
4 lebanese cucumbers (520g), seeded, sliced thinly
¼ cup (60ml) white wine vinegar
1 tablespoon white (granulated) sugar
1 teaspoon salt
1kg (2 pounds) kipfler (fingerling) potatoes, unpeeled, sliced diagonally
¼ cup (60ml) olive oil
1 cup loosely packed fresh dill sprigs
¼ cup (50g) rinsed, drained salted baby capers

1. Combine onion and cucumber in medium heatproof bowl.
2. Stir vinegar, sugar and salt over low heat in small saucepan, without boiling, until sugar is dissolved. Bring to the boil; pour over onion mixture, cool.
3. Meanwhile, boil, steam or microwave potato until tender; drain.
4. Place potato in large bowl with onion mixture, oil, dill and capers; toss gently to combine. Season to taste. Serve warm.

WARM KIPFLER AND CUCUMBER SALAD
with Dill

CHAPTER 5
Christmas
PUDDINGS
& DESSERTS

THE FIRST NOEL
the Angels Did Say

MAKE YOUR OWN
winter wonderland table decoration.
For this you will need a bell jar or a GLASS CAKE STAND
with a dome lid, a plate or plinth a little larger than the dome,
SOME FAKE SNOW (available online, search for fake snow)
and some SMALL CHRISTMAS DECORATIONS
such as a wooden house, fir trees, animals or small figurines
(available from Christmas shops).
MAKE UP A SMALL QUANTITY of fake snow by following packet instructions.
Arrange a 'hill' scene.
PLACE THE DOME on top to complete your
winter wonderland *decoration.*

THREE-IN-ONE Fruit Mix

PREP TIME 40 MINUTES (+ STANDING)

2⅓ cups (375g) sultanas
2 cups (300g) dried currants
2⅓ cups (375g) coarsely chopped raisins
1 cup (140g) finely chopped dried dates
¾ cup (125g) finely chopped seeded prunes
1 cup (190g) finely chopped dried figs
2 large apples (400g), grated coarsely
¼ cup (90g) golden syrup or treacle
2¼ cups (500g) firmly packed dark brown sugar
2 cups (500ml) brandy
2 teaspoons ground ginger
1 teaspoon each ground nutmeg and ground cinnamon

1 Combine ingredients in large bowl; cover tightly with plastic wrap. Store in a cool, dark place for a month (or longer, if desired) before using. Stir mixture every two or three days.

This basic fruit mix is enough to make a pudding (boiled or steamed) (recipe pages 200 & 201) large enough to serve 10 people, a regular-sized cake (recipe page 255) and a dozen mince pies (recipe page 303).

BOILED OR STEAMED PUDDING
(Three-in-One Fruit Mix)
(RECIPE PAGES 200 & 201)

BOILED OR STEAMED PUDDING
(Three-in-One Fruit Mix)

PREP + COOK TIME 5 HOURS 45 MINUTES (+ STANDING) **SERVES** 10

4¼ cups three-in-one fruit mix (page 197)
185g (6 ounces) butter, melted
2 eggs, beaten lightly
2 cups (140g) lightly packed stale breadcrumbs
¾ cup (110g) plain (all-purpose) flour

1 Place basic fruit mixture in large bowl. Stir in butter, eggs, breadcrumbs and sifted flour.

BOILED PUDDING

1 Fill a boiler three-quarters full with hot water, cover, bring to the boil. Have ready 2.5 metres (8 feet) of kitchen string and an extra ¾ cup (110g) plain flour. Wearing rubber gloves, dip prepared pudding cloth (see **TIPS**, page 201) into boiling water; boil for 1 minute. Remove cloth from water, squeeze excess water from cloth. Working quickly, spread hot cloth on bench, rub extra flour into centre of cloth to cover an area of about 40cm (16 inches) in diameter; leave flour a little thicker in centre of cloth where "skin" on pudding will need to be thickest.

2 Place pudding mixture in centre of cloth; gather cloth evenly around pudding, avoiding any deep pleats, pat into a round shape. Tie cloth tightly with string as close to mixture as possible. Knot corners of cloth together to make pudding easier to remove from boiler.

3 Gently lower pudding into boiling water. You may wish to tie free ends of string to handles of boiler to suspend pudding. Cover boiler with a tight-fitting lid; boil rapidly for 5 hours. Replenish boiling water as needed to maintain boil and water level; there must be enough boiling water for the pudding to be immersed at all times.

4 Untie pudding from handles. Place handle of wooden spoon through knotted cloth loops to lift pudding from water. Do not put pudding on bench; suspend from spoon on rungs of an upturned stool. Pudding must be suspended freely. If pudding has been cooked correctly, cloth will start to dry in patches within a few minutes; hang pudding for 10 minutes.

5 Place pudding on board, cut string; gently peel away cloth to uncover about half the pudding. Scrape skin back onto the pudding with a palette knife if necessary. Invert pudding onto a plate and continue to peel back cloth completely. Stand at least 20 minutes or until skin darkens and pudding becomes firm before cutting to serve.

STEAMED PUDDING

1. Grease 2-litre (8-cup) pudding steamer; line base with baking paper. Spoon pudding mixture into steamer. Place a 30cm x 40cm (12-inch x 16-inch) sheet of foil on bench, grease foil; top with a sheet of baking paper. Fold a 5cm (2-inch) pleat crossways through centre of both sheets.
2. Place sheets, baking-paper-side-down over steamer; secure firmly with kitchen string or steamer lid. Crush foil and baking paper firmly around rim to help form a good seal.
3. Place pudding in large boiler with enough boiling water to come halfway up side of steamer. Cover boiler with tight-fitting lid; steam 5 hours. Replenish with boiling water as necessary to maintain boil and water level during cooking. Stand pudding for 15 minutes before turning onto plate.

You need a 60cm (2-feet) square of unbleached calico for the boiled pudding cloth. If calico has not been used, soak it in cold water overnight. The next day, boil it for 20 minutes, then rinse it in cold water.

TO STORE PUDDING Wrap pudding thoroughly in plastic wrap then place in an airtight container or freezer bag. Refrigerate pudding for up to 3 months or freeze for a year.

TO DEFROST PUDDING Thaw frozen pudding for 2 days in the refrigerator. Remove from refrigerator 12 hours before reheating.

TO REHEAT STEAMED PUDDING Remove plastic wrap; return to steamer. Steam for 2 hours following the cooking instructions.

TO REHEAT BOILED PUDDING Remove plastic wrap and tie a clean, dry unfloured cloth around pudding. Boil for 2 hours following cooking instructions.

TO MICROWAVE To reheat the whole pudding, cover with microwave-safe plastic wrap; microwave on MEDIUM (50%) for about 15 minutes. To reheat four single serves at once, place on a microwave-safe plate, cover with microwave-safe plastic wrap; microwave on HIGH (100%) for about 3 minutes.

(PHOTOGRAPH PAGE 199)

STICKY FRUIT PUDDING
with Caramel Sauce

PREP + COOK TIME 3 HOURS 30 MINUTES (+ STANDING) **SERVES** 8

1½ cups (210g) coarsely chopped dried dates
1½ cups (375ml) water
1 teaspoon bicarbonate of soda (baking soda)
125g (4 ounces) butter, softened
1 teaspoon vanilla extract
1 cup (220g) firmly packed light brown sugar
3 eggs
1½ cups (225g) self-raising flour
1 cup (160g) mixed dried fruit, chopped finely

CARAMEL SAUCE
1 cup (220g) firmly packed light brown sugar
1¼ cups (310ml) thickened (heavy) cream
1 teaspoon vanilla extract
60g (2 ounces) butter, chopped coarsely
2 tablespoons brandy

1 Grease 2-litre (8-cup) pudding steamer.
2 Combine dates and the water in medium saucepan; bring to the boil, remove from heat. Add soda, stand 5 minutes. Blend or process date mixture until smooth; cool.
3 Beat butter, extract and sugar in small bowl with electric mixer until light and fluffy; beat in eggs, one at a time. Transfer mixture to large bowl, stir in date mixture, sifted flour and fruit; stand 15 minutes. Pour mixture into pudding steamer. Top with pleated baking paper and foil; secure with kitchen string or lid.
4 Place pudding in large saucepan with enough boiling water to come halfway up side of steamer. Cover with tight-fitting lid; boil 3 hours, adding boiling water as necessary to maintain water level.
5 Make caramel sauce.
6 Stand pudding 10 minutes before turning onto serving plate. Serve with caramel sauce.

CARAMEL SAUCE
Stir sugar, cream, extract and butter in medium saucepan over medium heat, until boiling. Reduce heat; simmer, uncovered, about 5 minutes or until thickened. Stir in brandy.

It is fine to use just one 300ml carton of cream for this recipe.
To make individual puddings: Spoon mixture into eight 1-cup (250ml) ovenproof dishes. Top with pleated baking paper and foil; secure with rubber bands. Place puddings in large, deep frying pan with enough boiling water to come halfway up side of dishes. Cover with tight-fitting lid. Boil 1 hour, adding boiling water as necessary to maintain water level. Stand puddings 5 minutes before turning out.

GOLDEN BOILED *Pudding*
(RECIPE PAGES 206 & 207)

GOLDEN BOILED
Pudding
(RECIPE PAGES 206 & 207)

GOLDEN BOILED
Pudding

PREP + COOK TIME 3 HOURS 40 MINUTES (+ STANDING) SERVES 16

1 cup (180g) finely chopped dried pears
1 cup (130g) finely chopped dried cranberries
1 cup (75g) finely chopped dried apples
½ cup (80g) finely chopped dried apricots
1 large apple (200g), peeled, grated coarsely
⅓ cup (80ml) orange-flavoured liqueur
2 teaspoons finely grated orange rind
2 tablespoons orange juice
250g (8 ounces) butter, softened
1½ cups (330g) caster (superfine) sugar
4 eggs
1 cup (150g) plain (all-purpose) flour
½ teaspoon bicarbonate of soda (baking soda)
1 teaspoon ground cinnamon
3 cups (210g) stale breadcrumbs
1 cup (120g) ground almonds
⅔ cup (100g) plain (all-purpose) flour, extra

1. Combine fruit, liqueur, rind and juice in large bowl. Cover, stand at room temperature overnight.
2. Beat butter and sugar in small bowl with electric mixer until combined; beat in eggs, one at a time. Mix butter mixture into fruit mixture. Mix in sifted flour, soda and cinnamon, then breadcrumbs and ground almonds.
3. Fill boiler three-quarters full of hot water, cover with tight-fitting lid; bring to the boil. Have ready 1-metre (1-yard) length of kitchen string and extra plain flour. Wearing thick rubber gloves, dip pudding cloth (see tips, page 207) into boiling water. Boil 1 minute then remove; squeeze excess water from cloth. Quickly spread hot cloth on bench. Rub extra flour into centre of cloth to cover an area about 40cm (16 inches) in diameter, leaving flour a little thicker in centre of cloth where "skin" on pudding needs to be thickest.

4. Place pudding mixture in centre of cloth. Gather cloth evenly around mixture, avoiding any deep pleats; pat into round shape. Tie cloth tightly with string as close to mixture as possible. Pull ends of cloth tightly to ensure pudding is as round and as firm as possible; tie loops in string.
5. Lower pudding into the boiling water; tie ends of string to handles of boiler to suspend pudding. Cover with a tight-fitting lid; boil 3 hours, adding boiling water as necessary to maintain water level.
6. Untie pudding from handles; place wooden spoon through string loops. Do not put pudding on bench; suspend from spoon by placing over rungs of upturned stool or wedging handle in a drawer. Twist ends of cloth around string to avoid them touching pudding; hang pudding for 10 minutes.
7. Place pudding on board; cut string, carefully peel back cloth. Turn pudding onto a plate then carefully peel cloth away completely. Stand at least 20 minutes or until skin darkens and pudding becomes firm. Serve dusted with icing sugar and drizzled with custard, if you like.

You need a 60cm (24-inch) square of unbleached calico for the pudding cloth. If calico has not been used before, soak it in cold water overnight; the next day, boil it for 20 minutes then rinse it in cold water.

We used Grand Marnier in this recipe but you could use any citrus-flavoured liqueur you like. This recipe will make two smaller puddings; use two 40cm (16-inch) squares of calico to make the smaller puddings. Boil puddings in separate boilers for 2 hours. If you only have one boiler, the pudding mixture will stand at room temperature while you cook the first one.

(PHOTOGRAPH PAGES 204 & 205)

FROZEN CHRISTMAS
Pudding
(RECIPE PAGES 210 & 211)

FROZEN CHRISTMAS *Pudding*

PREP + COOK TIME *2 HOURS* (+ COOLING, CHURNING & FREEZING) **SERVES 10**

1 vanilla bean
2½ cups (625ml) pouring cream
1 cup (250ml) milk
4 egg yolks
½ cup (110g) firmly packed light brown sugar

CHOCOLATE ORANGE ICE-CREAM
1¼ cups (310ml) pouring cream
¾ cup (180ml) milk
2 teaspoons finely grated orange rind
100g (3 ounces) finely chopped dark eating (semi-sweet) chocolate
3 egg yolks
⅓ cup (75g) caster (superfine) sugar
¼ cup (40g) sultanas
1 tablespoon rum or brandy
¼ cup (50g) quartered glacé cherries
¼ cup (40g) finely chopped mixed peel
50g (1½ ounces) finely chopped dark eating (semi-sweet) chocolate, extra

1 Grease 2-litre (8-cup) metal pudding basin. Line with plastic wrap; place in freezer.
2 To make brown sugar ice-cream, split vanilla bean in half lengthways, scrape seeds into medium saucepan. Add pod, cream and milk to pan; bring to the boil.
3 Meanwhile, whisk egg yolks and sugar in small bowl until pale; gradually whisk into hot cream mixture. Stir over low heat, without boiling, about 10 minutes or until mixture thickens and coats the back of a spoon. Strain custard into large heatproof bowl set over large bowl of ice; discard pod. Cover surface of custard with plastic wrap; stand until cold.
4 Pour custard into ice-cream maker, churn according to manufacturer's instructions (or follow instructions in **TIPS**, see right). Spoon ice-cream into pudding basin; freeze about 1 hour or until firm. Using a spatula, thickly coat inside of basin with ice-cream; cover with foil, return to freezer.
5 Meanwhile, make chocolate orange ice-cream.
6 Fill brown sugar ice-cream cavity with chocolate orange ice-cream; smooth surface. Cover with foil; freeze overnight.
7 Chill serving platter in freezer. Turn pudding basin onto platter; cover basin with a hot, damp cloth. Gradually pull plastic to ease pudding onto platter; discard plastic.

CHOCOLATE ORANGE ICE-CREAM
Bring cream, milk and rind to the boil in medium saucepan. Remove from heat, add chocolate; stir until smooth. Meanwhile, whisk egg yolks and sugar in small bowl until pale; gradually whisk into hot cream mixture. Stir over low heat, without boiling, about 10 minutes or until mixture thickens and coats the back of a spoon. Strain custard into large heatproof bowl set over bowl of ice. Cover surface with plastic wrap; stand until cold. Pour custard into ice-cream maker, churn according to manufacturer's instructions (or follow instructions in **TIPS**, see right). Spoon ice-cream into large bowl, stir in sultanas, rum, cherries, peel and extra chocolate.

If you don't have an ice-cream maker, pour custard mixture into shallow pan, cover with foil and freeze until almost set. Chop ice-cream roughly and beat in large bowl with electric mixer, or process, until smooth. Return to pan and freeze again, repeating process once more. Freeze about 1 hour, then allow to soften slightly; spoon ice-cream into pudding basin (or add additional ingredients) and follow the recipe. It's fine to use three 300ml cartons of pouring cream for this recipe, rather than buying an extra carton for the additional 35ml.

(PHOTOGRAPH PAGE 209)

When you have a food allergy or intolerance, particularly to gluten or dairy, then Christmas pudding is usually off the menu. Well not any more. And, as they say, the proof of the pudding (or steamed pudding as the case may be) is in the eating.

GLUTEN- AND DAIRY-FREE
Steamed Pudding

PREP + COOK TIME 6 HOURS 20 MINUTES SERVES 12

2¼ cups (360g) sultanas
1½ cups (240g) chopped raisins
½ cup (80g) dried currants
1½ cups (210g) coarsely chopped seeded dates
1½ cups (375ml) water
½ cup (125ml) orange juice
2 tablespoons honey
1 cup (220g) firmly packed light brown sugar
185g (6 ounces) dairy-free margarine
1 cup (125g) soya flour
1 cup (180g) rice flour
1 teaspoon cream of tartar
½ teaspoon bicarbonate of soda (baking soda)
2 teaspoons mixed spice
1 cup (120g) ground almonds

1. Combine fruit, the water, juice, honey, sugar and margarine in large saucepan. Stir over heat, without boiling, until margarine melts. Transfer mixture to large heatproof bowl; cool.
2. Grease 2.25-litre (9-cup) pudding steamer; line base with baking paper.
3. Stir sifted dry ingredients and ground almonds into fruit mixture.
4. Spoon mixture into steamer, cover with greased foil; secure with lid or kitchen string. Place steamer in large saucepan with enough boiling water to come halfway up side of steamer; simmer, covered, about 6 hours, replenishing with boiling water as necessary to maintain water level.
5. Stand pudding 10 minutes before turning onto serving plate.

CHOC-ORANGE Sauce

PREP + COOK TIME 15 MINUTES   MAKES 2 CUPS

400g (12½ ounces) dark eating (semi-sweet) chocolate, chopped coarsely
30g (1 ounce) butter, chopped coarsely
1 teaspoon vanilla extract
1 cup (250ml) pouring cream
2 tablespoons orange-flavoured liqueur

1 Stir chocolate and butter in medium heatproof bowl over medium saucepan of simmering water, until smooth.
2 Stir in extract, cream and liqueur. Serve warm.

SPICED RUM Butter

PREP TIME 10 MINUTES   MAKES 2½ CUPS

250g (8 ounces) unsalted butter, softened
½ cup (110g) firmly packed light brown sugar
2 teaspoons mixed spice
1½ teaspoons each ground cinnamon and ground ginger
large pinch each ground nutmeg and ground cloves
2 tablespoons dark rum

1 Beat butter in small bowl with electric mixer until as white as possible.
2 Beat in sugar, spices and rum until light and fluffy.

VANILLA BEAN Custard

PREP + COOK TIME 25 MINUTES   MAKES 2½ CUPS

1 vanilla bean
1¼ cups (310ml) pouring cream
¾ cup (180ml) milk
6 egg yolks
½ cup (110g) caster (superfine) sugar

1 Split vanilla bean in half lengthways; scrape seeds into medium saucepan, add pod, cream and milk. Bring to the boil then strain mixture into large jug. Discard pod.
2 Meanwhile, whisk egg yolks and sugar in medium heatproof bowl. Gradually whisk hot milk mixture into egg mixture.
3 Return custard mixture to pan; stir over low heat until mixture is thick enough to coat the back of a spoon. Serve warm or cold.

It is fine to use just one 300ml carton of cream for this recipe.

HAZELNUT Hard Sauce

PREP TIME 10 MINUTES   MAKES 1¾ CUPS

125g (4 ounces) unsalted butter, softened
1 cup (160g) icing (confectioners') sugar
2 tablespoons pouring cream
2 tablespoons hazelnut-flavoured liqueur

1 Beat butter and sifted sugar in small bowl with electric mixer until as white as possible.
2 Beat in cream and liqueur.

PISTACHIO MERINGUE
with White Peaches and Berries

PREP + COOK TIME 2 HOURS 15 MINUTES (+ COOLING) SERVES 10

2 cups (500ml) thickened (heavy) cream
4 medium white peaches (600g),
   cut into thin wedges
125g (4 ounces) fresh blueberries
125g (4 ounces) fresh blackberries
2 tablespoons coarsely chopped pistachios,
   roasted

PISTACHIO MERINGUE
1 cup (140g) coarsely chopped pistachios
6 egg whites
1½ cups (330g) caster (superfine) sugar
2 teaspoons cornflour (cornstarch)
2 teaspoons vanilla extract
2 teaspoons white vinegar

1. Make pistachio meringue.
2. Beat cream in small bowl with electric mixer until firm peaks form. Place one meringue on serving plate. Spread with half the cream; top with half the peaches and berries. Top with remaining meringue, cream, fruit and nuts.

PISTACHIO MERINGUE
Preheat oven to 120°C/250°F. Mark a 22cm (9-inch) circle on two sheets of baking paper. Turn paper over, place on two oven trays. Process half the nuts until fine. Beat egg whites in medium bowl with electric mixer until soft peaks form. Add sugar, a tablespoon at a time, beating until sugar dissolves between additions; beat until mixture is thick and glossy. Beat in cornflour, extract and vinegar; fold in ground nuts. Divide meringue mixture between circles on trays; spread evenly. Sprinkle with remaining nuts. Bake meringues about 1¼ hours. Cool meringues in oven with door ajar.

Make and assemble recipe at least a day ahead; this will make slicing it much easier.

Christmas Puddings & Desserts

FIG ALMOND AND
Mascarpone Trifle

PREP + COOK TIME 1 HOUR 15 MINUTES (+ COOLING & REFRIGERATION) **SERVES** 6

2 cups (500ml) water
1 cup (220g) caster (superfine) sugar
2 star anise
12 medium figs (720g), halved
¼ cup (60ml) almond-flavoured liqueur
12 sponge finger biscuits (140g)

ALMOND PRALINE
½ cup (70g) slivered almonds, roasted
½ cup (110g) caster (superfine) sugar
2 tablespoons water

ZABAGLIONE CREAM
4 eggs, separated
½ cup (110g) caster (superfine) sugar
⅓ cup (80ml) almond-flavoured liqueur
500g (1 pound) mascarpone cheese

1. Combine the water, sugar and star anise in large saucepan. Stir over heat until sugar is dissolved; bring to the boil. Add figs; simmer gently, uncovered, about 5 minutes or until tender. Cool; stir in liqueur. Remove figs from syrup; drain well. Reserve syrup. Place figs in large bowl.
2. Make almond praline.
3. Make zabaglione cream.
4. Dip one-third of the biscuits into fig syrup; place in single layer over 2-litre (8-cup) serving dish or in six 1-cup (250ml) serving glasses. Top with one-third of zabaglione cream, one-third poached figs and one-third almond praline. Repeat layering twice. Refrigerate at least 1 hour.

ALMOND PRALINE
Place nuts in single layer on greased oven tray. Combine sugar and the water in medium frying pan; stir over heat until sugar is dissolved. Bring to the boil; boil, uncovered, without stirring, until a deep golden colour. Allow bubbles to subside, pour over nuts; cool. Break praline into pieces.

ZABAGLIONE CREAM
Beat egg yolks and sugar in medium heatproof bowl with electric mixer over medium saucepan of simmering water until pale. Add liqueur; beat until mixture has tripled in volume and holds ribbon shapes when beaters are lifted. Cool. Place mascarpone in large bowl; beat until smooth. Fold in egg yolk mixture. Beat egg whites in small bowl with electric mixer until soft peaks form; fold into mascarpone mixture, in two batches.

PANETTONE WITH
Mascarpone and Raspberries

PANETTONE WITH
Mascarpone and Raspberries

PREP TIME 30 MINUTES (+ REFRIGERATION) **SERVES** 12

1 panettone (about 1.1kg)
¼ cup (60ml) orange-flavoured liqueur
750g (1½ pounds) fresh raspberries
2 teaspoons icing (confectioners') sugar

MASCARPONE FILLING
750g (1½ pounds) mascarpone cheese
¼ cup (40g) icing (confectioners') sugar
3 egg whites

1. Make mascarpone filling.
2. Using a serrated knife, cut domed top off panettone; reserve for another use. Split remaining panettone into three layers.
3. Place base of panettone onto serving plate. Sprinkle with 1 tablespoon of liqueur; spread with one-third of filling and scatter with one-third of the raspberries. Top with another slice of panettone. Repeat to make another two layers, finishing with mascarpone filling. Refrigerate, loosely covered.
4. Remove panettone from refrigerator 30 minutes before serving. Top with remaining raspberries; dust with sifted icing sugar.

MASCARPONE FILLING
Combine cheese and sifted sugar in large bowl. Beat egg whites in small bowl with electric mixer until soft peaks form. Fold egg whites into cheese mixture, in two batches.

We used Grand Marnier in this recipe but you could use any citrus-flavoured liqueur you like. This dessert is best made the day before or up to 5 hours before serving to allow the flavours to develop.
You can make it with all kinds of seasonal fruit such as mixed berries, sliced peaches, plums, nectarines or mango.
Store the reserved panettone in plastic wrap and toast for breakfast or make panettone toast (page 312).

WHITE CHRISTMAS
Ice-creams

PREP + COOK TIME 1 HOUR 15 MINUTES (+ COOLING & FREEZING) **MAKES** 8

1 vanilla bean
1¾ cups (430ml) milk
2⅓ cups (580ml) pouring cream
180g (5½ ounces) white eating chocolate, chopped
8 egg yolks
¾ cup (165g) caster (superfine) sugar
1 cup (130g) dried cranberries
2 tablespoons brandy
1 cup (140g) unsalted pistachios
2 teaspoons vegetable oil

1. Split vanilla bean lengthways; scrape seeds into medium saucepan. Add pod, milk, cream and 50g (1½ ounces) of the chocolate; bring to the boil.
2. Meanwhile, whisk egg yolks and sugar in medium bowl until thick and creamy; gradually whisk into hot milk mixture. Stir custard over low heat, without boiling, until thickened slightly. Cover surface of custard with plastic wrap; cool 20 minutes.
3. Strain custard into shallow container; discard pod. Cover with foil; freeze until almost firm.
4. Place custard in large bowl, chop coarsely; beat with electric mixer until smooth. Pour into deep container, cover; freeze until firm. Repeat process two more times.
5. Meanwhile, place cranberries and brandy in small bowl; stand 15 minutes.
6. Stir cranberry mixture and nuts into ice-cream. Spoon ice-cream into eight ¾-cup (180ml) moulds. Cover; freeze 3 hours or until firm.
7. Stir remaining chocolate and oil in small saucepan over low heat until mixture is smooth.
8. Dip each mould, one at a time, into a bowl of hot water for about 1 second. Turn ice-creams onto serving plates; top with warm chocolate mixture.

It is fine to use two 300ml (or one 600ml) cartons of cream for this recipe.

(PHOTOGRAPH PAGE 222)

WHITE CHRISTMAS
Ice-creams
(RECIPE PAGE 221)

HONEY PANNA COTTA WITH
Apricots in Thyme Syrup
(RECIPE PAGE 224)

HONEY PANNA COTTA WITH
Apricots in Thyme Syrup

PREP + COOK TIME 1 HOUR (+ COOLING & REFRIGERATION) SERVES 8

3 teaspoons gelatine
¼ cup (60ml) water
2⅓ cups (580ml) buttermilk
½ cup (125ml) pouring cream
½ cup (175g) honey

APRICOTS IN THYME SYRUP
2 cups (500ml) water
½ cup (175g) honey
2 teaspoons fresh thyme leaves
12 small apricots (600g), halved, seeded
1 tablespoon lemon juice

1. Sprinkle gelatine over the water in small heatproof jug; stand jug in small saucepan of simmering water, stir until gelatine dissolves.
2. Meanwhile, bring buttermilk and cream to the boil in medium saucepan; remove from heat. Whisk in honey and gelatine mixture; strain into large jug. Cool.
3. Divide buttermilk mixture among eight ⅔-cup (160ml) glasses. Refrigerate about 6 hours or overnight until set.
4. Make apricots in thyme syrup.
5. Serve panna cotta topped with apricots and syrup.

APRICOTS IN THYME SYRUP
Bring the water, honey and thyme to the boil in medium saucepan. Add apricots; simmer gently, uncovered, about 5 minutes or until almost tender. Remove from heat; add juice, cool. Refrigerate until cold.

(PHOTOGRAPH PAGE 223)

CHEAT'S FROZEN
Christmas Pudding

PREP TIME 30 MINUTES (+ FREEZING) SERVES 8

1 litre (4 cups) vanilla ice-cream, softened
700g (1½ pounds) golden fruit cake, crumbled
¼ cup (60ml) brandy or rum

1. Line eight ¾-cup (180ml) moulds with plastic wrap, extending plastic about 3cm (1¼ inches) over edge of moulds.
2. Process ice-cream, cake and brandy until combined. Spoon ice-cream mixture into moulds. Cover with plastic wrap then foil; freeze overnight.
3. Turn puddings onto a baking-paper-lined tray. Gently peel away plastic, transfer puddings to serving plates.

SERVING SUGGESTION
Serve with chocolate sauce or the choc-orange sauce on page 214.

ORANGE PUDDING
with Rum Sauce

PREP + COOK TIME 1 HOUR 30 MINUTES **SERVES** 8

1 large orange (300g)
10g (½ ounce) butter, melted
2 tablespoons light brown sugar
90g (3 ounces) butter, softened
¾ cup (165g) caster (superfine) sugar
2 teaspoons finely grated orange rind
2 eggs
1¼ cups (185g) self-raising flour
⅓ cup (50g) plain (all-purpose) flour
⅓ cup (125ml) milk

RUM SAUCE
50g (1½ ounces) butter
⅓ cup (115g) golden syrup or treacle
¼ cup (55g) firmly packed light brown sugar
2 tablespoons dark rum

1. Thinly slice unpeeled orange using a mandoline, V-slicer or sharp knife to 3mm (⅛-inch) thickness.
2. Brush 2-litre (8-cup) pudding steamer evenly with the melted butter. Sift brown sugar into steamer; shake to coat sides of steamer evenly with sugar. Arrange orange slices over bottom and around the side of the steamer so that the slices around the side touch the orange on the bottom of the steamer.
3. Beat softened butter, caster sugar and rind in small bowl with electric mixer until light and fluffy; beat in eggs, one at a time. Transfer mixture to medium bowl; stir in sifted flours and milk, in two batches.
4. Spoon mixture into steamer. Cover with pleated baking paper and foil; secure with lid. Place pudding steamer in large saucepan with enough boiling water to come halfway up side of steamer; cover pan with tight lid. Boil 1 hour, replenishing with boiling water as necessary to maintain water level. Stand pudding 5 minutes before turning out.
5. Meanwhile, make rum sauce.
6. Serve pudding with sauce.

RUM SAUCE
Stir butter, syrup and sugar in small saucepan over low heat until sugar dissolves; bring to the boil. Reduce heat; simmer, uncovered, 3 minutes or until thickened slightly. Remove from heat; stir in rum.

YULE Log

PREP + COOK TIME 1 HOUR 15 MINUTES (+ REFRIGERATION) **SERVES** 8

150g (4½ ounces) dark eating (semi-sweet) chocolate, melted
½ cup (75g) plain (all-purpose) flour
3 teaspoons each ground ginger and mixed spice
¼ teaspoon ground cloves
3 eggs
⅔ cup (150g) caster (superfine) sugar
¼ cup (60ml) hazelnut-flavoured liqueur
1 tablespoon icing (confectioners') sugar

HAZELNUT FILLING
250g (8 ounces) mascarpone cheese
250g (8 ounces) cream cheese, softened
¼ cup (25g) cocoa powder, sifted
½ cup (165g) chocolate hazelnut spread
¼ cup (60ml) hazelnut-flavoured liqueur

TUILE LEAVES
30g (1 ounce) butter, softened
¼ cup (55g) caster (superfine) sugar
1 egg white, beaten lightly
⅓ cup (50g) plain (all-purpose) flour

1 Preheat oven to 220°C/425°F. Grease two 25cm x 30cm (10-inch x 12-inch) swiss roll pans; line bases with baking paper, extending paper 5cm (2 inches) over long sides.

2 Spread chocolate in a thin layer in one of the pans. Refrigerate about 7 minutes or until chocolate is firm but slightly pliable. Tear chocolate into small pieces; refrigerate until required.

3 Meanwhile, sift flour and spices into small bowl. Beat eggs and ½ cup of the sugar in small bowl with electric mixer about 5 minutes or until thick and creamy. Transfer to large bowl; sift flour mixture over egg mixture, then fold into the egg mixture. Pour into pan; bake about 15 minutes. Reduce oven to 180°C/350°F.

4 Place large sheet of baking paper on wire rack; sprinkle paper with remaining sugar. Turn cake onto baking paper, remove lining paper, immediately roll up cake from short side; cool.

5 Meanwhile, make hazelnut filling; reserve 1½ cups. Make tuile leaves.

6 Unroll cake, brush with liqueur; spread with remaining filling, leaving a 3cm (1¼-inch) border on one short side. Roll up from opposite short side, using paper as a guide. Transfer to serving platter. Spread reserved filling over cake. Decorate with chocolate pieces. Using a skewer make spiral patterns on each end of log. Refrigerate 1 hour. Dust log with sifted icing sugar just before serving. Decorate log with tuile leaves.

HAZELNUT FILLING
Beat ingredients in small bowl with electric mixer until thick and creamy.

TUILE LEAVES
Using a leaf-shaped cutter as a template, trace around cutter on thick cardboard. Cut out the centre of the shape, leaving a stencil. Line oven tray with baking paper. Stir butter and sugar in medium bowl; stir in egg white. Stir in sifted flour until smooth. Drop 1 teaspoon of mixture into leaf cut-out on tray. Spread mixture thinly to make leaf. Carefully lift template from leaf, position on tray about 3cm (1¼ inches) away from the first leaf. (Make and bake three leaves at a time.) Bake in 180°C/350°F oven about 8 minutes or until browned lightly. Working quickly, slide a spatula under tuile to loosen, then place over a rolling pin to form curved shapes. Cool on rolling pin 5 minutes before transferring to wire rack to cool. Repeat with remaining mixture.

TIRAMISU
Torte

PREP + COOK TIME 1 HOUR 10 MINUTES (+ COOLING & REFRIGERATION) SERVES 12

3 eggs
½ cup (110g) caster (superfine) sugar
¼ cup (35g) plain (all-purpose) flour
¼ cup (35g) self-raising flour
¼ cup (35g) pure cornflour (cornstarch)
2 tablespoons instant coffee granules
¾ cup (180ml) boiling water
⅓ cup (80ml) marsala
2 tablespoons coffee-flavoured liqueur
500g (1 pound) mascarpone cheese
⅓ cup (55g) icing (confectioners') sugar
1¼ cups (300ml) thickened (heavy) cream

1 Preheat oven to 180°C/350°F. Grease deep 22cm (9-inch) square cake pan with butter.
2 Beat eggs in small bowl with electric mixer about 10 minutes or until thick and creamy; gradually add caster sugar, one tablespoon at a time, beating until sugar dissolves between additions. Transfer to large bowl.
3 Sift flours twice. Sift flours over egg mixture; fold ingredients together. Spread mixture into pan.
4 Bake sponge about 25 minutes. Turn sponge immediately onto baking-paper-covered wire rack, turn top-side up to cool.
5 Meanwhile, dissolve coffee in the water in small heatproof jug. Stir in marsala and liqueur; cool.
6 Beat mascarpone and icing sugar in small bowl with electric mixer until smooth. Beat in cream and ⅓ cup of the coffee mixture.
7 Split sponge in half vertically then each sponge in half horizontally. Place one of the cake rectangles on serving plate, cut-side up; brush with a quarter of the remaining coffee mixture then spread with ⅔ cup of mascarpone mixture. Repeat layering process finishing with the cake, cut-side down, and remaining mascarpone mixture spread on top and sides of cake. Refrigerate cake 2 hours.
8 Decorate cake with coarsely chopped vienna almonds, if you like.

It is fine to use just one 300ml carton of cream for this recipe.
Alternate the sponge pieces when layering so that the cut side of the sponge is on different sides on each layer; this will ensure the torte is even and does not lean to one side.
Vienna almonds are toffee-coated almonds; they're available from specialist nut shops.

FRUIT MINCE TART
with White Chocolate Cream

PREP + COOK TIME *1 HOUR 45 MINUTES (+ REFRIGERATION)* **SERVES 8**

75g (2½ ounces) cold unsalted butter, chopped coarsely
1 cup (150g) plain (all-purpose) flour
½ cup (80g) pure icing (confectioners') sugar
1 egg yolk
1 teaspoon vanilla extract
1 tablespoon iced water
60g (2 ounces) white eating chocolate
2 teaspoons cocoa powder

FRUIT MINCE
410g (13 ounces) bottled fruit mince
½ cup (65g) dried cranberries
1 medium green apple (150g), grated coarsely
1 tablespoon brandy
1 teaspoon finely grated lemon rind

WHITE CHOCOLATE CREAM
2 teaspoons gelatine
2 tablespoons boiling water
3 eggs, separated
¼ cup (55g) caster (superfine) sugar
180g (5½ ounces) white eating chocolate, melted
1¼ cups (310ml) thickened (heavy) cream, whipped

1. Make fruit mince and white chocolate cream.
2. Blend or process butter, and sifted flour and icing sugar until crumbly. Add egg yolk, extract and the water; process until ingredients come together. Enclose in plastic wrap; refrigerate 30 minutes.
3. Roll pastry between sheets of baking paper until large enough to line 11cm x 35cm (4½-inch x 14-inch) rectangular loose-based flan tin. Lift pastry into tin, press into sides, trim excess; prick base all over with a fork. Cover; refrigerate 20 minutes.
4. Meanwhile, preheat oven to 200°C/400°F.
5. Place tin on oven tray; line pastry with baking paper then fill with dried beans or rice. Bake 15 minutes. Remove beans and paper; bake about 15 minutes or until pastry is browned. Cool.
6. Spread fruit mince into pastry case. Top with white chocolate cream. Refrigerate 1 hour or overnight. Using a vegetable peeler, shave chocolate over cream, dust with sifted cocoa.

FRUIT MINCE
Combine ingredients in small bowl.

WHITE CHOCOLATE CREAM
Sprinkle gelatine over the water in small heatproof jug; stir until gelatine dissolves, cool 5 minutes. Whisk egg yolks and sugar in large bowl. Fold in cooled chocolate and gelatine mixture. Beat two of the egg whites in small bowl with electric mixer until soft peaks form (discard remaining egg white or reserve for another use). Fold egg white into chocolate mixture, in two batches; fold in cream. Cover; refrigerate 30 minutes.

It is fine to use just one 300ml carton of cream for this recipe.

LEMON AND RASPBERRY *Semifreddo*

PREP + COOK TIME 1 HOUR 15 MINUTES (+ FREEZING) SERVES 12

2 tablespoons finely grated lemon rind
½ cup (125ml) lemon juice
1 cup (220g) caster (superfine) sugar
8 egg yolks
¼ cup (60ml) limoncello liqueur
2⅓ cups (580ml) thickened (heavy) cream
1 cup (150g) frozen raspberries, crumbled coarsely
60g (2 ounces) fresh raspberries
fresh mint sprigs

CANDIED LEMON SLICES
1 medium lemon (140g), sliced thinly
¼ cup (55g) caster (superfine) sugar
¾ cup (180ml) water

1. Grease 9cm x 25cm (3½-inch x 10-inch) loaf pan. Line with baking paper, extending paper 5cm (2 inches) over edges of pan.
2. Stir rind, juice and sugar in small saucepan until sugar is dissolved; bring to the boil. Remove from heat, cool 10 minutes. Strain lemon syrup into small jug; discard solids.
3. Beat egg yolks in small bowl with electric mixer until light and fluffy. Beat in lemon syrup and liqueur; transfer to large bowl.
4. Beat cream in medium bowl with electric mixer until soft peaks form. Fold cream into lemon mixture, cover bowl with foil; freeze about 4 hours or until thick.
5. Stir frozen raspberries into cream mixture; pour into loaf pan. Cover with plastic wrap then foil; freeze overnight or until firm.
6. Meanwhile, make candied lemon slices.
7. Stand semifreddo at room temperature 5 minutes before turning out. Top with candied lemon, fresh raspberries and mint.

CANDIED LEMON SLICES
Place lemon in small saucepan, cover with cold water. Bring to the boil; simmer, uncovered, 1 minute, drain. Combine sugar and the water in small saucepan; stir over low heat until sugar dissolves. Add lemon slices, bring to the boil; remove from heat. Stand 30 minutes or until slices are translucent; drain. Place lemon slices on wire rack over tray; cool. Store, covered with baking paper, at room temperature.

Limoncello liqueur is an Italian lemon-flavoured liqueur made from the peel only of fragrant lemons. The peels are steeped in a good-quality clear alcohol then diluted with sugar and water. Available from good liquor outlets and Italian food stores.

HAZELNUT MUD CAKE
with Fudge Frosting

PREP + COOK TIME 2 HOURS (+ COOLING) SERVES 12

360g (11½ ounces) dark eating (semi-sweet) chocolate, chopped coarsely
225g (7 ounces) butter, chopped coarsely
¾ cup (165g) firmly packed light brown sugar
¾ cup (180ml) water
¾ cup (110g) plain (all-purpose) flour
¼ cup (35g) self-raising flour
½ cup (50g) ground hazelnuts
2 eggs
⅓ cup (80ml) hazelnut-flavoured liqueur

FUDGE FROSTING
45g (1½ ounces) butter, chopped coarsely
1 tablespoon water
⅓ cup (75g) firmly packed light brown sugar
2 tablespoons hazelnut-flavoured liqueur
1 cup (160g) icing (confectioners') sugar
2 tablespoons cocoa powder

1 Preheat oven to 150°C/300°F. Grease deep 20cm (8-inch) round cake pan; line base and side with baking paper.
2 Stir chocolate, butter, sugar and the water in medium saucepan over low heat until smooth. Cool 15 minutes.
3 Stir sifted flours, ground hazelnuts, eggs and liqueur into chocolate mixture. Pour into pan.
4 Bake about 1 hour 35 minutes. Stand cake in pan 5 minutes; turn, top-side up, onto wire rack to cool.
5 Meanwhile, make fudge frosting.
6 Spread cake with frosting.

FUDGE FROSTING
Stir butter, the water and brown sugar in small saucepan over heat until sugar dissolves. Remove from heat; stir in liqueur. Sift icing sugar and cocoa into small bowl; gradually stir in hot butter mixture until smooth. Cover; refrigerate about 15 minutes or until frosting thickens. Beat frosting with a wooden spoon until spreadable.

We used Frangelico for this recipe, but you can use any hazelnut or chocolate-flavoured liqueur you like.

CHAPTER 6
Christmas
CAKES

SILENT NIGHT
Holy Night

CREATE FALLING SNOWFLAKES with various white doilies.
YOU WILL NEED at least 12 lace or fabric doilies,
a bottle of fabric stiffener to harden the doilies (available from craft stores),
a small foam roller and tray (from the hardware store), newspaper,
baking paper, scissors and WHITE OR SILVER RIBBON.
Lay the newspaper on a flat surface and top with two long sheets
of baking paper to cover the length of the surface.
LAY THE DOILIES in the middle of the baking paper leaving a gap between each one.
Place some stiffener in the tray and using the roller, coat a doily thoroughly.
Flip over and repeat on the underside.
LEAVE TO DRY OVERNIGHT or until totally dry and hardened.
Cut 12 different lengths of WHITE OR SILVER RIBBON
and tie one end to the doily, threading it through a hole in the lace trim.
Attach masking tape to the other end of the ribbon, hang half of the doilies to the top of
THE WINDOW FRAME and the remaining doilies to the curtain rail.
This will give you two rows of falling
snowflakes.

GRAND MARNIER
Fruit Cake
(RECIPE PAGES 244 & 245)

GRAND MARNIER
Fruit Cake
(RECIPE PAGES 244 & 245)

GRAND MARNIER
Fruit Cake

PREP + COOK TIME 5 HOURS 40 MINUTES (+ STANDING & COOLING)

3 cups (500g) sultanas
1½ cups (250g) mixed peel
¾ cup (120g) coarsely chopped raisins
¾ cup (120g) coarsely chopped seeded dried dates
⅔ cup (140g) coarsely chopped seeded prunes
½ cup (125g) coarsely chopped glacé apricots
⅔ cup (150g) coarsely chopped glacé pineapple
½ cup (70g) slivered almonds
½ cup (60g) coarsely chopped walnuts
1 tablespoon finely grated orange rind
½ cup (110g) caster (superfine) sugar
¼ cup (60ml) orange juice
½ cup (125ml) Grand Marnier
250g (8 ounces) butter, softened
½ cup (110g) firmly packed light brown sugar
5 eggs
2 cups (300g) plain (all-purpose) flour
2 tablespoons Grand Marnier, extra
1kg (2 pounds) ready-made white icing
1 egg white, beaten lightly
½ cup (80g) pure icing (confectioners') sugar, sifted
25cm (10-inch) round covered cake board
decorative ribbon
silver cachous

1 Combine fruit, nuts and rind in large bowl.
2 Cook caster sugar in large frying pan over low heat, without stirring, until it begins to melt, then stir until sugar is melted and browned lightly. Remove from heat, slowly stir in juice; return to low heat, stir until toffee dissolves (do not boil). Stir in liqueur.
3 Pour syrup over fruit mixture. Cover with plastic wrap; store mixture in a cool, dark place for 10 days, stirring every day.
4 Preheat oven to 150°C/300°F. Line base and sides of deep 22cm (9-inch) round or deep 20cm (8-inch) square cake pan with one layer of brown paper and two layers of baking paper, extending papers 5cm (2 inches) above edge.

5 Beat butter and brown sugar in small bowl with electric mixer until just combined; beat in eggs, one at a time. Stir butter mixture into fruit mixture. Mix in sifted flour; spread mixture into pan. Tap pan firmly on bench to settle mixture into pan; level cake mixture with wet spatula.

6 Bake cake about 3½ hours. Remove cake from oven, brush with extra liqueur; cover hot cake with foil then turn upside down to cool overnight.

7 Trim top of cake with sharp knife to ensure it sits flat when turned upside down. Mix a little white icing and cold boiled water to a sticky paste. Spread about 2 tablespoons of this mixture into the centre of a sheet of baking paper about 5cm (2 inches) larger than the cake; position cake upside down on paper.

8 Using spatula and small pieces of white icing, patch any holes on cake.

9 Brush egg white evenly over cake. Knead white icing on surface dusted with icing sugar until smooth; roll to 6mm (¼-inch) thickness. Lift icing onto cake with rolling pin, smoothing icing over cake with hands dusted with icing sugar. Using sharp knife, cut excess icing away from base of cake.

10 Mix scraps of white icing and cold boiled water to a sticky paste. Spread about 2 tablespoons of paste in centre of board; centre cake on prepared board. Move the cake to the correct position on the board; using sharp craft knife or scalpel, carefully cut away excess baking paper extending around base of cake.

11 Secure ribbon around cake using pins (remove before cutting cake). Push cachous gently into icing in the design of your choice.

(PHOTOGRAPH PAGES 242 & 243)

NIGHT BEFORE
Fruit Cake
(RECIPE PAGE 248)

'Twas the night before Christmas... and you forgot the fruit cake. Head straight to the kitchen with this recipe: it doesn't require weeks of soaking dried fruit and it's out of the oven in 45 minutes – perfect. Cut it up on Christmas Day and no one will know the difference.

NIGHT BEFORE
Fruit Cake

PREP + COOK TIME 1 HOUR 15 MINUTES (+ COOLING) MAKES 24

1½ cups (240g) mixed dried fruit
⅓ cup (60g) finely chopped glacé ginger
410g (13 ounces) bottled fruit mince
175g (5½ ounces) butter, chopped coarsely
⅔ cup (150g) firmly packed light brown sugar
1 teaspoon finely grated lemon rind
2 tablespoons lemon juice
½ cup (125ml) brandy
½ teaspoon bicarbonate of soda (baking soda)
3 eggs, beaten lightly
½ cup (140g) mashed banana
1½ cups (225g) plain (all-purpose) flour
½ cup (75g) self-raising flour
½ cup (70g) slivered almonds

1 Combine fruit, ginger, fruit mince, butter, sugar, rind, juice and ⅓ cup of the brandy in medium saucepan; stir over heat until butter is melted and sugar dissolved. Bring to the boil, remove from heat; stir in soda. Transfer to large bowl; cool.

2 Preheat oven to 160°C/325°F. Grease 20cm x 30cm (8-inch x 12-inch) rectangular pan; line base and two long sides with baking paper, extending paper 5cm (2 inches) above sides.

3 Stir egg and banana into fruit mixture, then stir in sifted flours. Spread mixture into pan; sprinkle with nuts.

4 Bake cake about 45 minutes. Brush hot cake with remaining brandy, cover with foil; cool in pan. Cut cake into 24 squares. Dust with sifted icing (confectioners') sugar to serve, if you like.

You need 1 large (230g) overripe banana to get the amount of mashed banana required for this recipe.

(PHOTOGRAPH ALSO PAGE 246)

RICH CHOCOLATE
Fruit Cake

PREP + COOK TIME 3 HOURS 50 MINUTES (+ STANDING & REFRIGERATION) SERVES 20

850g (1¾ pounds) canned seeded black cherries in syrup
1 cup (150g) raisins, chopped coarsely
¾ cup (120g) finely chopped seeded dried dates
½ cup (80g) sultanas
½ cup (95g) finely chopped seeded prunes
1 cup (200g) dried figs, chopped finely
1 cup (250ml) marsala
1 cup (120g) pecans
185g (6 ounces) butter, softened
2 teaspoons finely grated orange rind
1¼ cups (275g) firmly packed dark brown sugar
3 eggs
1¼ cups (185g) plain (all-purpose) flour
½ cup (75g) self-raising flour
2 tablespoons cocoa powder
2 teaspoons mixed spice
100g (3 ounces) dark eating (semi-sweet) chocolate, chopped finely

GANACHE
200g dark eating (semi-sweet) chocolate, chopped coarsely
½ cup (125ml) pouring cream

1. Drain cherries; reserve ⅓ cup syrup. Quarter cherries. Combine cherries with remaining fruit, ¾ cup of the marsala and reserved cherry syrup in large bowl. Cover; stand overnight.
2. Preheat oven to 150°C/300°F. Grease deep 22cm (9-inch) round cake pan; line with two layers of baking paper, extending paper 5cm (2 inches) over edge of pan.
3. Process half the nuts until ground finely; chop the remaining nuts coarsely.
4. Beat butter, rind and sugar in small bowl with electric mixer until combined; beat in eggs, one at a time. Mix butter mixture into fruit mixture; stir in sifted dry ingredients, chocolate and ground and chopped nuts. Spread mixture into pan.
5. Bake cake about 3 hours. Brush hot cake with remaining marsala, cover with foil; cool in pan.
6. Make ganache.
7. Spread cake with ganache; top with chocolate decoration (see tips below). Dust with sifted icing (confectioners') sugar to serve, if you like.

GANACHE
Stir ingredients in small saucepan over low heat until smooth. Refrigerate, stirring occasionally, about 20 minutes or until spreadable.

Store un-iced cake in the refrigerator for up to 3 months. Once iced, the cake can be stored in the fridge for 2 weeks. Cut and bring to room temperature before serving.
We painted a branch of real holly roughly with melted dark chocolate to make the inedible decoration on the cake. Remove cake from fridge, then top with the chocolate decoration.

IRISH PUDDING *Cake*

PREP + COOK TIME *4 HOURS (+ STANDING & COOLING)* **SERVES 8**

1½ cups (250g) seeded dried dates, chopped coarsely
1½ cups (250g) raisins, chopped coarsely
1¼ cups (200g) seeded prunes, chopped coarsely
1 cup (150g) dried currants
¾ cup (125g) sultanas
1 large apple (200g), grated coarsely
1½ cups (375ml) irish whiskey
1¼ cups (275g) firmly packed light brown sugar
185g (6 ounces) butter, softened
3 eggs, beaten lightly
½ cup (50g) ground hazelnuts
1½ cups (225g) plain (all-purpose) flour
1 teaspoon ground nutmeg
½ teaspoon bicarbonate of soda (baking soda)
½ teaspoon each ground ginger and ground cloves

1 Combine fruit and 1 cup of the whiskey in large bowl. Cover with plastic wrap; stand overnight.
2 Preheat oven to 120°C/250°F. Grease deep 20cm (8-inch) round cake pan; line with two layers of baking paper, extending paper 5cm (2 inches) over edge of pan.
3 Stir remaining whiskey and ½ cup of the sugar in small saucepan over heat until sugar dissolves; bring to the boil. Cool syrup 20 minutes.
4 Meanwhile, beat butter and remaining sugar in small bowl with electric mixer until just combined (do not overbeat). Beat in eggs, one at a time. Add butter mixture to fruit mixture; stir in ground hazelnuts, sifted dry ingredients and ½ cup of the cooled syrup. Spread mixture into pan.
5 Bake cake about 3½ hours. Brush cake with reheated remaining syrup, cover cake with foil; cool in pan.

If your dilemma is whether to make a Christmas cake or pudding, this recipe is the best of both possible worlds because it's just as delicious served hot as a pudding or cold as a cake. And it's not necessary to make it ages in advance: starting to prepare it a day or so ahead is just fine. It will keep, covered, in the refrigerator for several months. Although the inclusion of irish whiskey makes it authentic, scotch, dark rum or brandy are fine substitutes.

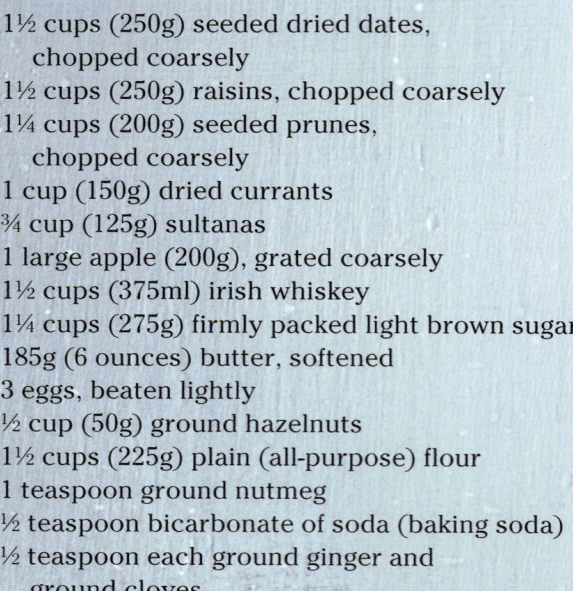

FRUIT CAKE
(Three-in-One Fruit Mix)

PREP + COOK TIME 3 HOURS (+ COOLING) **SERVES** 20

4¼ cups three-in-one fruit mix (page 197)
185g (6 ounces) butter, melted
3 eggs, beaten lightly
1½ cups (225g) plain (all-purpose) flour
½ teaspoon bicarbonate of soda (baking soda)
¼ cup (60ml) brandy

1 Preheat oven to 140°C/280°F. Line base and side of deep 20cm (8-inch) round cake pan with one layer of brown paper and two layers of baking paper, extending paper 5cm (2 inches) over edge of pan.
2 Place fruit mix in large bowl. Stir in butter, eggs and sifted flour and soda. Spread mixture into pan; level top.
3 Bake cake about 2½ hours. Brush hot cake with brandy. While still hot, cover cake, still in its pan, tightly with foil, then wrap in a towel and cool overnight.

Turn cake out of pan, remove lining paper from side of cake. Wrap tightly in plastic wrap. Place cake in an airtight container to protect it. Store in the refrigerator for up to 3 months, or freeze for up to a year. Thaw frozen cake in the refrigerator for 2 days.

WHITE CHRISTMAS
Slice

PREP TIME 20 MINUTES (+ REFRIGERATION) **MAKES** 32

500g (1 pound) white eating chocolate, chopped coarsely
1 cup (35g) rice bubbles
1 cup (160g) sultanas
1 cup (80g) desiccated coconut
⅔ cup (110g) finely chopped dried apricots
½ cup (100g) halved red glacé cherries

1 Grease 20cm x 30cm (8-inch x 12-inch) rectangular pan; line base and long sides with baking paper, extending paper 5cm (2 inches) above sides.
2 Melt chocolate in large heatproof bowl set over large saucepan of simmering water. Remove from heat; quickly stir in remaining ingredients.
3 Press mixture firmly into pan. Refrigerate 2 hours or until firm.

(PHOTOGRAPH PAGE 256)

Christmas Cakes

WHITE CHRISTMAS
Slice

(RECIPE PAGE 255)

GLUTEN-FREE FRUIT
and Almond Loaves
(RECIPE PAGE 258)

GLUTEN-FREE FRUIT
and Almond Loaves

PREP + COOK TIME 2 HOURS 35 MINUTES
(+ STANDING & COOLING) MAKES 2

1kg (2 pounds) mixed dried fruit
1 tablespoon finely grated orange rind
⅔ cup (160ml) sweet sherry
150g (4½ ounces) butter, softened
⅔ cup (150g) firmly packed dark brown sugar
4 eggs
100g (3 ounces) marzipan, chopped coarsely
1 small apple (130g), grated coarsely
¾ cup (100g) ground almonds
1¼ cups (185g) gluten-free plain (all-purpose) flour
1 cup (160g) blanched almonds
¼ cup (60ml) sweet sherry, extra

1 Combine fruit, rind and sherry in large bowl; mix well. Cover with plastic wrap; stand in cool, dark place for one week, stirring every day.
2 Preheat oven to 150°C/300°F. Line bases and sides of two 9cm x 21cm (3¼-inch x 8½-inch) loaf pans with two layers of baking paper, extending paper 5cm (2 inches) above sides.
3 Beat butter and sugar in small bowl with electric mixer until just combined. Beat in eggs, one at a time. Mix butter mixture into fruit mixture. Stir in marzipan, apple, ground almonds and sifted flour. Spread mixture into pans; decorate with nuts.
4 Bake loaves about 2 hours. Brush hot loaves with extra sherry, cover with foil; cool in pans.

(PHOTOGRAPH PAGE 257)

GOLDEN GLACE
Fruit Cake

PREP + COOK TIME 4 HOURS (+ COOLING)
SERVES 20

150g (5 ounces) glacé pear, chopped finely
150g (5 ounces) red and green glacé cherries, chopped finely
150g (5 ounces) glacé peach, chopped finely
125g (4 ounces) glacé ginger, chopped finely
125g (4 ounces) glacé figs, chopped finely
⅔ cup (160ml) brandy or orange-flavoured liqueur
250g (8 ounces) unsalted butter, softened
1 cup (220g) caster (superfine) sugar
4 eggs
1⅔ cups (250g) plain (all-purpose) flour
1 cup (120g) ground almonds

1 Preheat oven to 150°C/300°F. Line base and side of deep 20cm (8-inch) round cake pan with one layer of brown paper and two layers of baking paper, extending paper 5cm (2 inches) over edge of pan.
2 Combine fruit and ½ cup of the brandy in large bowl.
3 Beat butter and sugar in small bowl with electric mixer until combined. Beat in eggs one at a time. Add butter mixture to fruit mixture; mix well. Stir in sifted flour and ground almonds, in two batches. Spread mixture into pan; smooth top.
4 Bake cake about 3 hours. Brush hot cake with remaining brandy. While still hot, cover cake, still in its pan, tightly with foil; cool in pan.

Cake will keep in an airtight container for up to a month. Cake can be frozen for 3 months.

Christmas Cakes

CHOCOLATE DRAMBUIE
Fruit Cake

PREP + COOK TIME 4 HOURS 50 MINUTES (+ STANDING & COOLING) SERVES 36

2⅓ cups (375g) sultanas
2¼ cups (335g) raisins, chopped coarsely
1⅔ cups (270g) dried currants
1½ cups (250g) seeded prunes, chopped coarsely
1½ cups (210g) seeded dried dates, chopped coarsely
¾ cup (125g) mixed peel
⅔ cup (140g) red glacé cherries, quartered
1⅓ cups (330ml) Drambuie
⅓ cup (120g) honey
1 tablespoon finely grated lemon rind
250g (8 ounces) butter, softened
1½ cups (330g) firmly packed dark brown sugar
6 eggs
90g (3 ounces) dark eating (semi-sweet) chocolate, grated coarsely
1¼ cups (150g) pecans, chopped coarsely
2 cups (300g) plain (all-purpose) flour
1 cup (150g) self-raising flour
¼ cup (25g) cocoa powder
1 cup (125g) pecan halves
6 glacé cherries

1. Combine fruit, 1 cup of the liqueur, honey and rind in large bowl. Cover with plastic wrap; stand in cool, dark place for one week, stirring every day.
2. Preheat oven to 120°C/250°F. Grease six-hole (¾-cup/180ml) texas muffin pan. Grease deep 22cm (9-inch) round or deep 20cm (8-inch) square cake pan; line base and side(s) with four layers of baking paper, extending paper 5cm (2 inches) above side(s).
3. Beat butter and sugar in medium bowl with electric mixer until just combined. Beat in eggs, one at a time. Mix butter mixture into fruit mixture with chocolate and nuts. Stir in sifted dry ingredients, in two batches.
4. Fill each muffin pan hole, level to the top, with mixture; spread remaining mixture into cake pan. Decorate tops with pecans and glacé cherries.
5. Bake muffins 1½ hours (cake can stand while muffins are baking). Brush hot muffins with some of the remaining liqueur, cover with foil; cool in pan.
6. Increase oven to 150°C/300°F; bake large cake 3 hours. Brush hot cake with remaining liqueur, cover with foil; cool in pan.

If you don't want to make the muffins, spread all the cake mixture into a deep 25cm (10-inch) round or deep 22cm (9-inch) square cake pan, and bake about 4 to 4½ hours.
Cake can be made up to 3 months ahead; store in an airtight container in the refrigerator, or freeze for up to a year.

CELEBRATION
Christmas Cakes

PREP + COOK TIME 3 HOURS 15 MINUTES (+ STANDING & COOLING) MAKES 2

3 cups (500g) sultanas
1¾ cups (300g) raisins
1¾ cups (300g) seeded dried dates
1 cup (150g) dried currants
¼ cup (40g) candied orange
⅔ cup (130g) red glacé cherries
¼ cup (55g) glacé ginger
¼ cup (60g) dried apricots
½ cup (125ml) orange-flavoured liqueur
250g (8 ounces) butter, softened
1 cup (220g) firmly packed light brown sugar
5 eggs
1½ cups (225g) plain (all-purpose) flour
⅓ cup (50g) self-raising flour
1 teaspoon mixed spice
2 tablespoons orange-flavoured liqueur, extra
1kg (2 pounds) ready-made white icing
1 egg white
½ cup (80g) icing (confectioners') sugar
20cm (8-inch) square cake board
silver cachous
silver ribbon

1. Chop all fruit the same size as a sultana. Combine fruit and liqueur in large bowl; cover with plastic wrap, stand overnight.
2. Preheat oven to 150°C/300°F. Line two deep 15cm (6-inch) square cake pans with three layers of baking paper, extending paper 5cm (2 inches) above sides of pans.
3. Beat butter and brown sugar in small bowl with electric mixer until combined; beat in eggs, one at a time. Mix butter mixture into fruit mixture. Stir in sifted flours and spice; divide mixture between pans.
4. Bake cakes about 2 hours. Brush hot cakes with extra liqueur, cover with foil, turn upside down on bench; cool in pan.
5. Trim top of one cake if necessary to make it flat. Mix a walnut-sized piece of white icing with enough cold boiled water to make a sticky paste. Spread half of this mixture into the centre of a sheet of baking paper about 5cm (2 inches) larger than the cake; position cake top-side down on paper. Using spatula and small pieces of white icing, patch any holes in the cake.
6. Brush egg white evenly over cake. Knead half the remaining white icing on surface dusted with sifted icing sugar until smooth; roll to 6mm (¼-inch) thickness. Lift icing onto cake with rolling pin, smoothing icing over cake with hands dusted with icing sugar. Cut excess icing away from base of cake.
7. Mix icing scraps with cold boiled water to make a sticky paste. Spread half the paste in centre of cake board; centre cake on board. Cut away excess baking paper around base of cake.
8. Gently push a 6cm (2½-inch) bell-shaped cutter three-quarters of the way into icing. Using a small sharp knife, carefully remove about half the icing inside the bell shape. Carefully pull cutter out of icing. Push cachous gently into icing to fill bell. Secure half the ribbon around cake using pins. Repeat with second cake.

CHOCOLATE AND SHERRY *Cherry Cake*

PREP + COOK TIME 1 HOUR 50 MINUTES (+ STANDING & COOLING) MAKES 2 (EACH CAKE SERVES 6)

- 300g (9½ ounces) fresh cherries, seeded, quartered
- ½ cup (125ml) sweet sherry
- 100g (3 ounces) butter, chopped coarsely
- 200g (6½ ounces) dark eating (semi-sweet) chocolate, chopped coarsely
- 1⅓ cups (300g) firmly packed light brown sugar
- 4 eggs
- ⅔ cup (100g) self-raising flour
- ½ cup (50g) cocoa powder
- ⅓ cup (80g) sour cream

CHOCOLATE GANACHE
- 200g (6½ ounces) dark eating (semi-sweet) chocolate, chopped coarsely
- ½ cup (125ml) pouring cream
- 1 tablespoon glucose syrup

1. Combine cherries and sherry in small bowl; cover, stand at room temperature 3 hours or overnight.
2. Preheat oven to 160°C/325°F. Grease two deep 15cm (6-inch) square cake pans; line bases and sides with baking paper, extending paper 5cm (2 inches) over sides.
3. Melt butter and chocolate in medium heatproof bowl over medium saucepan of simmering water. Remove from heat; stir in sugar. Using electric mixer, beat in eggs, one at a time. Add sifted dry ingredients; beat on low speed until combined. Beat in sour cream, then stir in cherry mixture. Pour mixture evenly into pans.
4. Bake cakes about 1 hour 20 minutes; cool cakes in pans.
5. Make chocolate ganache.
6. Place cakes on serving plates; spread ganache over cakes.

CHOCOLATE GANACHE
Stir ingredients in small heatproof bowl over small pan of simmering water until smooth. Stand about 20 minutes or until spreadable.

Glucose helps give the ganache a glossy look. Glucose syrup is available from most supermarkets in the baking aisle.
Cakes may be stored in an airtight container in the refrigerator for up to a month, or frozen for up to 3 months. The ganache will not be as glossy after freezing.

GLUTEN- AND DAIRY-FREE
Spicy Fruit Cake

PREP + COOK TIME 3 HOURS (+ STANDING & COOLING) SERVES 20

1¼ cups (200g) sultanas
1 cup (150g) finely chopped seeded dried dates
1 cup (150g) raisins, chopped coarsely
¾ cup (120g) dried currants
1 cup (250g) coarsely chopped glacé apricots
1 cup (250ml) tokay
185g (6 ounces) dairy-free margarine
1 cup (220g) firmly packed dark brown sugar
3 eggs
1 cup (120g) ground almonds
1½ cups (270g) rice flour
1 teaspoon cream of tartar
½ teaspoon bicarbonate of soda (baking soda)
1 teaspoon ground nutmeg
½ teaspoon each ground ginger and ground cloves

1 Combine fruit and ¾ cup of the tokay in large bowl; cover with plastic wrap; stand overnight.
2 Preheat oven to 120°C/250°F. Line deep 22cm (9-inch) round cake pan with two layers of baking paper, extending paper 5cm (2 inches) above side.
3 Beat margarine and sugar in small bowl with electric mixer until combined; beat in eggs, one at a time. Mix butter mixture into fruit mixture; mix in ground almonds and sifted dry ingredients. Spread mixture into pan.
4 Bake cake about 2½ hours. Brush hot cake with remaining tokay, cover with foil; cool in pan. Serve dusted with sifted pure icing (confectioners') sugar, if you like.

Tokay is a sweet white fortified wine.
Store cake in the refrigerator for up to 3 months. Cut the cake straight from the fridge, then bring to room temperature before serving.

FRUIT MINCE
Friands

BOILED FRUIT
Cake

FRUIT MINCE
Friands

PREP + COOK TIME 35 MINUTES MAKES 12

6 egg whites
185g (6 ounces) unsalted butter, melted
1 teaspoon finely grated orange rind
1 cup (120g) ground almonds
1½ cups (240g) icing (confectioners') sugar
½ cup (75g) plain (all-purpose) flour
½ cup (150g) bottled fruit mince

1. Preheat oven to 180°C/350°F. Grease 12-hole (½-cup/125ml) oval friand pan.
2. Whisk egg whites in medium bowl until frothy. Stir in butter, rind, ground almonds, then sifted icing sugar and flour. Spoon mixture into pan holes.
3. Bake friands 10 minutes. Remove friands from oven; press a small, 1cm (½-inch) deep hole in top of each friand with the end of a wooden spoon. Spoon fruit mince into holes; bake about 10 minutes.
4. Stand friands in pan 5 minutes before turning, top-side up, onto wire rack to cool. Serve dusted with sifted icing (confectioners') sugar.

BOILED FRUIT
Cake

PREP + COOK TIME 3 HOURS 50 MINUTES (+ COOLING) SERVES 20

3 cups (450g) raisins, chopped coarsely
1½ cups (240g) sultanas
¾ cup (120g) dried currants
½ cup (100g) red glacé cherries, chopped coarsely
¼ cup (60ml) brandy
250g (8 ounces) butter, chopped coarsely
1 cup (250ml) water
½ cup (110g) firmly packed dark brown sugar
½ cup (110g) caster (superfine) sugar
½ teaspoon bicarbonate of soda (baking soda)
4 eggs, beaten lightly
1¼ cups (185g) self-raising flour
1¼ cups (185g) plain (all-purpose) flour
1 cup (120g) pecans
¾ cup (100g) macadamias
¼ cup (60ml) brandy, extra

1. Combine fruit, brandy, butter, the water, sugars and soda in large saucepan; stir over heat until butter is melted and sugar dissolved. Bring to the boil; remove from heat, transfer to large bowl. Cool mixture to room temperature.
2. Preheat oven to 150°C/300°F. Grease deep 22cm (9-inch) round or deep 20cm (8-inch) square cake pan; line base and side(s) of pan with two layers of baking paper, extending paper 5cm (2 inches) above side(s).
3. Stir egg into fruit mixture, then stir in sifted flours; spread mixture into pan. Decorate top with nuts.
4. Bake cake about 3 hours. Brush hot cake with extra brandy, cover with foil; cool in pan.

JOY TO THE
World

RED AND WHITE LOLLIES
look really festive arranged in
different jars on a mantelpiece or WINDOW SILL.
YOU WILL NEED a selection of red and white lollies
from your local sweet shop, a selection of clean JAM JARS
or medicine jars with lids, and tongs.
Wash the jam jars or MEDICINE JARS to remove any labels and dry well.
Arrange the sweets in LAYERS OR COLOURS in the jars
and top with lids.
Place a pair of tongs *nearby.*

GINGERBREAD
House

(RECIPE PAGES 276 & 277)

GINGERBREAD *House*

PREP + COOK TIME 3 HOURS 30 MINUTES (+ REFRIGERATION & STANDING)   MAKES 1 HOUSE (SERVES 20)

paper, for house template
2¼ cups (335g) self-raising flour
1½ teaspoons ground ginger
1 teaspoon ground cinnamon
¾ teaspoon ground cloves
½ teaspoon ground nutmeg
90g (3 ounces) butter, chopped coarsely
½ cup (110g) firmly packed dark brown sugar
¼ cup (90g) treacle
1 egg, beaten lightly
4 large bamboo skewers
1¼ cups (185g) milk chocolate melts, melted
½ cup (110g) caster (superfine) sugar
2 tablespoons water
cooking-oil spray
2 tablespoons coarsely chopped dried cranberries
1 tablespoon coarsely chopped pistachios
1¼ cups (185g) white chocolate melts, melted
35cm (14-inch) round or square cake board
3 cups (360g) whole pecans
1½ cups (120g) desiccated coconut
2 teaspoons icing (confectioners') sugar

1 Cut paper templates for gingerbread house: two 13cm x 17.5cm (5¼-inch x 7-inch) rectangles for the roof, two 10cm x 15.5cm (4-inch x 6¼-inch) rectangles for the side walls, and two 10cm x 18cm (4-inch x 7¼-inch) rectangles for the front and back walls. Trim front and back walls to make two 10cm (4-inch) high gables. Cut two 3.5cm (1½-inch) windows from each side wall. Cut door out of one side wall, reserving door cut-out piece. Cut out a 3.5cm (1½-inch) square for window sills.

2 Process flour, spices and butter until crumbly. Add brown sugar, treacle and egg; process until combined. Turn dough onto floured surface; knead until smooth. Cover with plastic wrap; refrigerate 1 hour.

3 Preheat oven to 180°C/350°F.

4 Roll dough, in several batches, between sheets of baking paper until 5mm (¼-inch) thick. Peel away top paper and use templates to cut shapes from dough. Remove excess dough. Slide baking paper with shapes onto oven trays.

5 Bake about 12 minutes or until shapes are barely firm (they become crisp when cool).

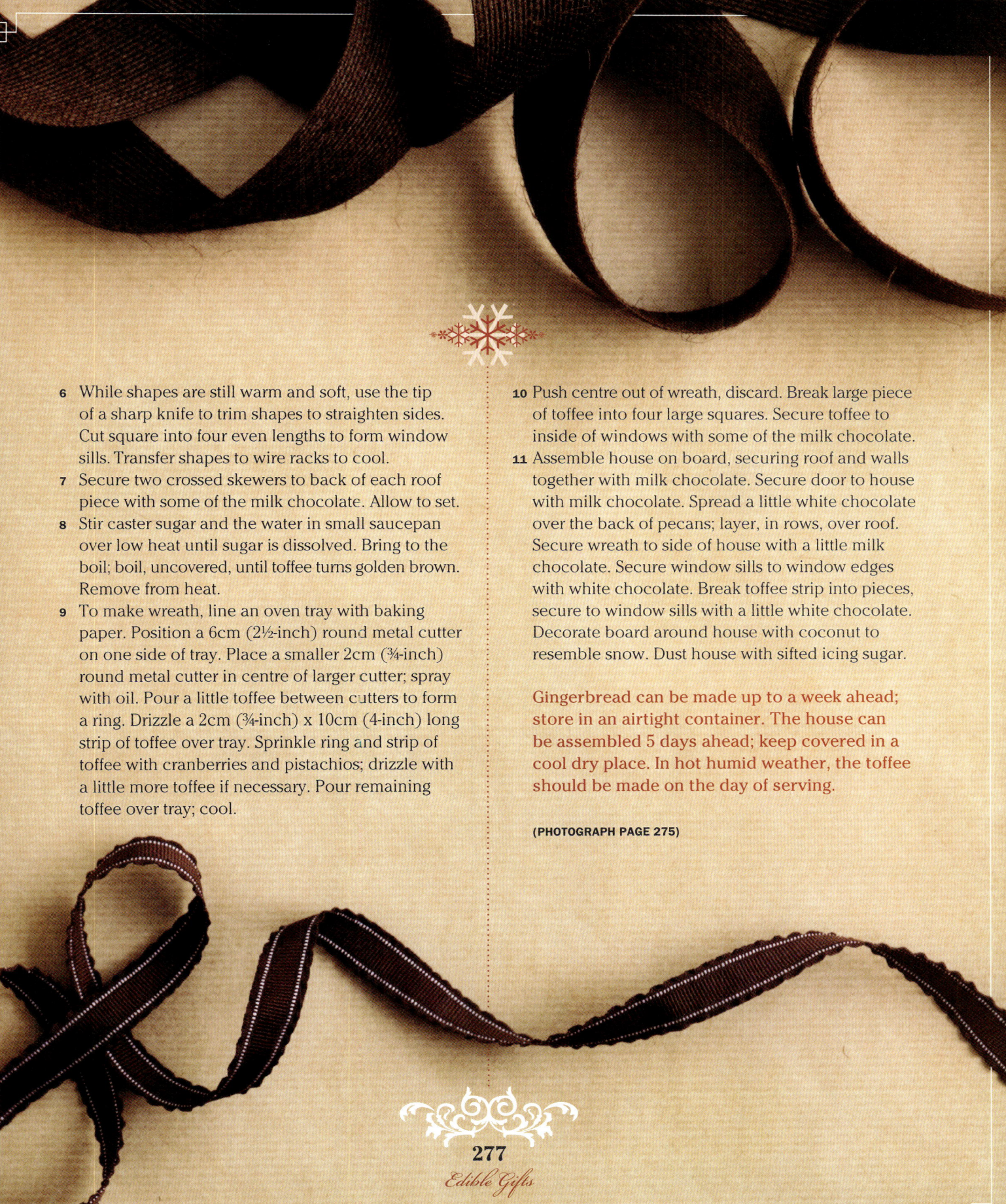

6. While shapes are still warm and soft, use the tip of a sharp knife to trim shapes to straighten sides. Cut square into four even lengths to form window sills. Transfer shapes to wire racks to cool.
7. Secure two crossed skewers to back of each roof piece with some of the milk chocolate. Allow to set.
8. Stir caster sugar and the water in small saucepan over low heat until sugar is dissolved. Bring to the boil; boil, uncovered, until toffee turns golden brown. Remove from heat.
9. To make wreath, line an oven tray with baking paper. Position a 6cm (2½-inch) round metal cutter on one side of tray. Place a smaller 2cm (¾-inch) round metal cutter in centre of larger cutter; spray with oil. Pour a little toffee between cutters to form a ring. Drizzle a 2cm (¾-inch) x 10cm (4-inch) long strip of toffee over tray. Sprinkle ring and strip of toffee with cranberries and pistachios; drizzle with a little more toffee if necessary. Pour remaining toffee over tray; cool.
10. Push centre out of wreath, discard. Break large piece of toffee into four large squares. Secure toffee to inside of windows with some of the milk chocolate.
11. Assemble house on board, securing roof and walls together with milk chocolate. Secure door to house with milk chocolate. Spread a little white chocolate over the back of pecans; layer, in rows, over roof. Secure wreath to side of house with a little milk chocolate. Secure window sills to window edges with white chocolate. Break toffee strip into pieces, secure to window sills with a little white chocolate. Decorate board around house with coconut to resemble snow. Dust house with sifted icing sugar.

Gingerbread can be made up to a week ahead; store in an airtight container. The house can be assembled 5 days ahead; keep covered in a cool dry place. In hot humid weather, the toffee should be made on the day of serving.

(PHOTOGRAPH PAGE 275)

MINI CHRISTMAS *Puddings*

PREP + COOK TIME 2 HOURS 50 MINUTES (+ STANDING) MAKES 6

1 cup (150g) raisins, chopped coarsely
1 cup (160g) sultanas
1 cup (150g) finely chopped seeded dried dates
½ cup (95g) finely chopped seeded prunes
½ cup (85g) mixed peel
½ cup (125g) finely chopped glacé apricots
1 teaspoon finely grated lemon rind
2 tablespoons lemon juice
2 tablespoons apricot jam
2 tablespoons brandy
250g (8 ounces) butter, softened
2 cups (440g) firmly packed light brown sugar
5 eggs
1¼ cups (185g) plain (all-purpose) flour
½ teaspoon ground nutmeg
½ teaspoon mixed spice
4 cups (280g) stale breadcrumbs
1 cup (150g) plain (all-purpose) flour, extra
6 x 30cm (12-inch) squares unbleached calico

1. Combine fruit, rind, juice, jam and brandy in large bowl. Cover with plastic wrap; stand in cool, dark place for one week, stirring every day.
2. Beat butter and sugar in small bowl with electric mixer until combined; beat in eggs, one at a time. Stir butter mixture into fruit mixture. Stir in sifted dry ingredients and breadcrumbs.
3. Fill boiler three-quarters full of hot water, cover with tight lid; bring to the boil. Have ready 1-metre (1-yard) length of kitchen string and extra flour. Wearing thick rubber gloves, dip pudding cloths, one at a time, into boiling water; boil 1 minute then remove, squeeze excess water from cloth. Spread hot cloths on bench; rub 2 tablespoons of the extra flour into centre of each cloth to cover an area about 18cm (7¼ inches) in diameter, leaving flour a little thicker in centre of cloth where "skin" on the pudding needs to be thickest.
4. Divide pudding mixture equally among cloths; placing in centre of each cloth. Gather cloths around mixture, avoiding any deep pleats; pat into round shapes. Tie cloths tightly with string as close to mixture as possible. Tie loops in string. Lower three puddings into the boiling water. Cover, boil 2 hours, replenishing with boiling water as necessary to maintain water level.
5. Lift puddings from water using wooden spoons through string loops. Do not put puddings on bench; suspend from spoon by placing over rungs of an upturned stool or wedging the spoon in a drawer. Twist ends of cloth around string to avoid them touching puddings; hang 10 minutes. Repeat with remaining puddings.
6. Place puddings on board; cut string, carefully peel back cloth. Turn puddings onto plates then carefully peel cloth away completely. Stand at least 20 minutes or until skin darkens and pudding becomes firm.

Top puddings with a slice of glacé orange, if you like. It is available from gourmet and health-food stores.
If the six 30cm (12-inch) squares of unbleached calico have not been used before, soak them in cold water overnight; the next day, boil them for 20 minutes then rinse in cold water. Puddings can be cooked in two boilers or in batches; the mixture will keep at room temperature for several hours.

BROWNIE
Bombs

PREP + COOK TIME 1 HOUR (+ COOLING & REFRIGERATION) **MAKES** 50

Preheat oven to 180°C/350°F. Grease deep 20cm (8-inch) square cake pan; line base and sides with baking paper. Stir 125g (4 ounces) chopped butter and 200g (6½ ounces) chopped dark eating (semi-sweet) chocolate in medium saucepan over low heat until smooth; transfer to large bowl, cool 10 minutes. Stir in ⅔ cup caster (superfine) sugar, 2 lightly beaten eggs and 1¼ cups sifted plain (all-purpose) flour. Spread mixture into pan; bake about 30 minutes. Cool in pan. Cut brownie into large pieces; process with ⅓ cup dark rum until mixture comes together. Roll heaped teaspoons of mixture into balls. Freeze for 10 minutes. Melt 200g (6½ ounces) chopped dark eating (semi-sweet) chocolate; dip balls into chocolate to coat. Refrigerate until set. Drizzle with 60g (2 ounces) melted white chocolate, decorate with pieces of glacé cherry.

CHRISTMAS
Cookies

PREP + COOK TIME 30 MINUTES (+ REFRIGERATION) **MAKES** 28

Grease oven trays; line with baking paper. Beat 250g (8 ounces) softened butter, ¾ cup caster (superfine) sugar and 1 egg in small bowl with electric mixer until light and fluffy; transfer to large bowl. Stir in 2¼ cups sifted plain (all-purpose) flour. Knead dough on floured surface until smooth. Cover; refrigerate 30 minutes. Preheat oven to 180°C/350°F. Roll heaped teaspoons of mixture into 15cm (6-inch) log shapes. Twist two pieces of dough together, shape into canes and wreaths. Place on trays. Bake about 12 minutes; cool on trays. Sprinkle hot cookies with 2 tablespoons cinnamon sugar.

CHRISTMAS Muffins

PREP + COOK TIME 40 MINUTES MAKES 12

Preheat oven to 200°C/400°F. Grease 12-hole (⅓-cup/80ml) muffin pan. Sift 2½ cups self-raising flour into medium bowl; rub in 100g (3 ounces) chopped butter. Gently stir in 1 cup caster (superfine) sugar, 1¼ cups buttermilk and 1 beaten egg. Gently stir in 1 cup mixed coarsely chopped glacé fruit. Spoon mixture into pan holes; bake about 20 minutes. Stand muffins 5 minutes before turning, top-side up, onto wire rack to cool. Roll 250g (8 ounces) ready-made white icing out to 5mm (¼-inch) thick; cut out 12 x 4.5cm (1¾-inch) stars. Brush tops of muffins with 2 tablespoons warmed, strained apricot jam; top with icing stars. Dust with sifted icing (confectioners') sugar, if you like.

FRUIT NUT Clusters

PREP + COOK TIME 30 MINUTES (+ REFRIGERATION) MAKES 36

Line three 12-hole patty pans with paper patty cases. Stir 150g (4½ ounces) chopped butter, ½ cup caster (superfine) sugar and 2 tablespoons honey in small saucepan over low heat until sugar dissolves. Combine 3½ cups cornflakes, ½ cup coarsely chopped dried cranberries, ½ cup roasted flaked almonds, ½ cup coarsely chopped roasted pistachios and ⅓ cup finely chopped glacé peach in large bowl. Stir in butter mixture. Spoon mixture into paper cases; refrigerate until set.

PASSIONFRUIT
Cream Biscuits

PREP + COOK TIME 45 MINUTES (+ REFRIGERATION & COOLING) MAKES 25

125g (4 ounces) butter, softened
2 teaspoons finely grated lemon rind
⅓ cup (75g) caster (superfine) sugar
2 tablespoons golden syrup or treacle
1 cup (150g) self-raising flour
⅔ cup (100g) plain (all-purpose) flour
¼ cup (60ml) passionfruit pulp

PASSIONFRUIT CREAM
2 tablespoons passionfruit pulp
90g (3 ounces) butter, softened
1 cup (160g) icing (confectioners') sugar

1. Beat butter, rind and sugar in small bowl with electric mixer until light and fluffy. Add golden syrup, beat until combined. Stir in sifted dry ingredients and passionfruit pulp.
2. Turn dough onto floured surface, knead gently until smooth. Divide dough in half; roll each portion between sheets of baking paper to 5mm (¼-inch) thickness. Refrigerate 30 minutes.
3. Preheat oven to 180°C/350°F. Grease oven trays; line with baking paper.
4. Cut 25 x 4cm (1½-inch) fluted rounds from each portion of dough; place about 2.5cm (1 inch) apart on trays.
5. Bake biscuits about 10 minutes. Cool on trays.
6. Meanwhile, make passionfruit cream.
7. Spoon passionfruit cream into piping bag fitted with 5mm (¼-inch) fluted tube. Pipe cream onto half the biscuits; top with remaining biscuits. Serve dusted with a little extra sifted icing sugar, if you like.

PASSIONFRUIT CREAM
Strain passionfruit pulp through fine sieve into small jug, discard seeds. Beat butter and sugar in small bowl with electric mixer until light and fluffy. Beat in passionfruit juice.

You need about six passionfruit for this recipe.

FRUIT MINCE PIES WITH SPICED
Hazelnut Pastry

PREP + COOK TIME 1 HOUR (+ REFRIGERATION & COOLING) MAKES 18

1½ cups (225g) plain (all-purpose) flour
¾ cup (75g) ground hazelnuts
½ cup (80g) icing (confectioners') sugar
2 teaspoons mixed spice
185g (6 ounces) cold butter, chopped coarsely
1 egg yolk
2 teaspoons iced water, approximately
1½ cups (375g) bottled fruit mince
2 teaspoons finely grated orange rind
1 egg, beaten lightly

1. Process flour, ground hazelnuts, sugar, spice and butter until crumbly. With motor operating, add egg yolk and enough of the water to make ingredients come together. Turn dough onto floured surface, knead gently until smooth. Cover with plastic wrap; refrigerate 30 minutes.
2. Preheat oven to 220°C/425°F. Grease 18 holes of two 12-hole (2-tablespoons/40ml) deep flat-based patty pans.
3. Divide pastry in half. Roll one portion between sheets of baking paper until 5mm (¼-inch) thick. Cut out nine 7.5cm (3-inch) fluted rounds; press rounds into holes. Repeat with remaining pastry.
4. Combine fruit mince and rind in medium bowl; spoon mince mixture into cases, brush edge of pastry with egg. Roll scraps of pastry on floured surface until 5mm (¼-inch) thick. Cut out 18 x 5cm (2-inch) fluted rounds; cut 2cm (¾-inch) fluted round from centre of each. Top pies with rounds.
5. Bake pies about 25 minutes. Stand pies 10 minutes; turn, top-side up, onto wire rack to cool. Dust with a little extra sifted icing sugar.

MACADAMIA AND PECAN
Shortbread

PREP + COOK TIME 45 MINUTES MAKES 24

250g (8 ounces) butter, softened
½ cup (110g) caster (superfine) sugar
2 teaspoons vanilla extract
2 cups (300g) plain (all-purpose) flour
½ cup (75g) rice flour
⅓ cup (45g) finely chopped macadamias
½ cup (60g) finely chopped pecans
2 tablespoons caster (superfine) sugar, extra

1. Preheat oven to 160°C/325°F. Lightly grease two oven trays.
2. Beat butter, sugar and extract in small bowl with electric mixer until pale and fluffy. Transfer mixture to large bowl; stir in sifted flours and nuts, in two batches. Press mixture together. Turn dough onto lightly floured surface; knead gently until smooth.
3. Divide dough in half. Roll each portion between sheets of baking paper into 23cm (9-inch) rounds; place on trays. Mark each round into 12 wedges, prick with a fork. Using floured fingers, pinch a frill around each shortbread, sprinkle with extra sugar.
4. Bake shortbread about 20 minutes. Stand on trays 10 minutes before transferring to wire racks to cool.

Use a cake pan or plate to mark, then cut the dough into a neat round.
Shortbread will keep in an airtight container for up to a month.

(PHOTOGRAPH PAGE 288)

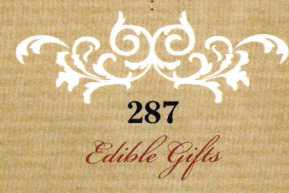

MACADAMIA AND PECAN
Shortbread
(RECIPE PAGE 287)

STAINED GLASS
Christmas Cookies
(RECIPE PAGE 290)

STAINED GLASS Christmas Cookies

PREP + COOK TIME 50 MINUTES (+ REFRIGERATION) **MAKES** 32

1 vanilla bean
250g (8 ounces) butter, softened
¾ cup (165g) caster (superfine) sugar
1 egg
1 tablespoon water
2¼ cups (335g) plain (all-purpose) flour
90g (3 ounces) individually wrapped sugar-free fruit drops, assorted colours

1 Split vanilla bean lengthways; scrape seeds into medium bowl with butter, sugar, egg and the water. Beat with electric mixer until combined. Stir in sifted flour, in two batches. Knead dough on floured surface until smooth. Cover with plastic wrap; refrigerate 30 minutes.
2 Preheat oven to 180°C/350°F. Line two oven trays with baking paper.
3 Using a rolling pin, gently tap the wrapped lollies to crush them slightly. Unwrap lollies, separate by colour into small bowls.
4 Roll dough between sheets of baking paper to 5mm (¼-inch) thickness. Cut shapes from dough using 8cm (3¼-inch) long Christmas tree cutter; place cookies on oven trays. Using a 4cm (1½-inch) long Christmas tree or 1.5cm (¾-inch) star cutter, cut out the centre of each tree to make windows. Use a skewer to make a small hole in top of each tree for threading through ribbon, if you like.
5 Bake trees 7 minutes. Remove trays from oven; fill each window with a few of the same-coloured lollies. Bake a further 5 minutes or until browned lightly. Cool trees on trays.

(PHOTOGRAPH PAGE 289)

SEA SALT AND Cashew Caramels

PREP + COOK TIME 30 MINUTES (+ COOLING) **MAKES** 40

1½ cups (330g) caster (superfine) sugar
1½ cups (375ml) thickened (heavy) cream
¼ cup (90g) glucose syrup
1½ cups (225g) unsalted roasted cashews
2 teaspoons sea salt

1 Grease an 18cm x 28cm (7¼-inch x 11¼-inch) slice pan. Line base and sides with baking paper, extending paper 5cm (2 inches) over sides.
2 Stir sugar, cream and glucose in medium saucepan until sugar is dissolved. Bring to the boil; boil, uncovered, until mixture reaches 120°C (248°F) on a candy thermometer.
3 Add nuts and half the salt, do not stir. Pour caramel into pan; sprinkle with remaining salt. Cool.
4 Use a warm oiled sharp knife to cut caramel into pieces.

Glucose syrup is available from most supermarkets in the baking aisle.
Store caramels between layers of baking paper in an airtight container in a cool dry place for up to a week.
When packaging as a gift, layer between sheets of baking paper.

SEA SALT AND
Cashew Caramels

ANGEL GIFT TAG Cookies

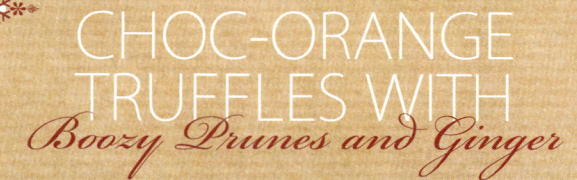

PREP + COOK TIME 50 MINUTES (+ REFRIGERATION & STANDING)
MAKES 20

125g (4 ounces) butter, softened
¾ cup (165g) caster (superfine) sugar
1 egg
1¾ cups (260g) plain (all-purpose) flour
⅓ cup (50g) self-raising flour
2 tablespoons white (granulated) sugar
red ribbon

LEMON ROYAL ICING
2 cups (320g) pure icing (confectioners') sugar
1 egg white
2 teaspoons lemon juice

1. Beat butter, caster sugar and egg in small bowl with electric mixer until light and fluffy. Stir in sifted flours, in two batches. Knead dough on floured surface until smooth. Cover with plastic wrap; refrigerate 30 minutes.
2. Preheat oven to 180°C/350°F. Line two oven trays with baking paper.
3. Roll dough between sheets of baking paper to 5mm (¼-inch) thickness. Cut 20 x 8cm x 11cm (3¼-inch x 4½-inch) angel shapes from dough; cut two 2cm (¾-inch) moon shapes across centre of angel shapes for threading ribbon. Place on oven trays.
4. Bake cookies about 12 minutes. Cool on trays.
5. Meanwhile, make lemon royal icing.
6. Spread angel cookies with icing; sprinkle with sugar crystals. Stand at room temperature until icing is set; thread ribbon through holes.

LEMON ROYAL ICING
Sift icing sugar through fine sieve onto sheet of baking paper. Beat egg white in small bowl with electric mixer until foamy; beat in icing sugar, a tablespoon at a time. Stir in juice.

Store cookies in an airtight container for up to 2 days to keep them crisp until you want to attach them to your gifts.

CHOC-ORANGE TRUFFLES WITH Boozy Prunes and Ginger

PREP + COOK TIME 1 HOUR (+ STANDING & REFRIGERATION) **MAKES 24**

½ cup (125ml) thickened (heavy) cream
450g (14½ ounces) dark eating (semi-sweet) chocolate, chopped coarsely
½ cup (50g) cocoa powder

BOOZY PRUNES AND GINGER
⅓ cup (60g) finely chopped seeded prunes
2 tablespoons finely chopped glacé ginger
2 teaspoons finely grated orange rind
1 tablespoon orange-flavoured liqueur

1. Make boozy prunes and ginger.
2. Combine cream and chocolate in medium heatproof bowl. Place bowl over medium saucepan of simmering water; stir until mixture is smooth. Stand at room temperature until mixture starts to thicken. Stir in prune mixture. Refrigerate about 2 hours or until firm.
3. Sift cocoa into medium bowl. Roll level tablespoons of chocolate mixture into balls; roll in cocoa. Place on tray; refrigerate until firm.
4. Remove from refrigerator 30 minutes before serving. Dust with a little extra sifted cocoa.

BOOZY PRUNES AND GINGER
Combine ingredients in small bowl; cover, stand overnight.

Grand Marnier or Cointreau can be used for the orange-flavoured liqueur.
Store truffles in an airtight container in the refrigerator for up to 3 weeks. Truffles, without cocoa coating, can be frozen for up to 3 months. Remove from freezer 1 hour before serving.

(PHOTOGRAPH PAGE 294)

CHOC-ORANGE TRUFFLES WITH
Boozy Prunes and Ginger
(RECIPE PAGE 293)

CHOCOLATE
Fig Panforte
(RECIPE PAGE 296)

CHOCOLATE Fig Panforte

PREP + COOK TIME 1 HOUR 10 MINUTES (+ STANDING)   **SERVES** 20

¾ cup (110g) plain (all-purpose) flour
2 tablespoons cocoa powder
2 teaspoons ground cinnamon
1¾ cups (150g) coarsely chopped semi-dried figs
¼ cup (40g) finely chopped glacé orange
1 cup (160g) blanched almonds, roasted
1 cup (140g) hazelnuts, roasted
1 cup (120g) pecans, roasted
⅓ cup (115g) honey
⅓ cup (75g) caster (superfine) sugar
⅓ cup (75g) firmly packed light brown sugar
2 tablespoons water
100g (3 ounces) dark eating (semi-sweet) chocolate, melted

1. Preheat oven to 150°C/300°F. Grease deep 20cm (8-inch) round cake pan; line base with baking paper.
2. Sift flour, cocoa and cinnamon into large bowl; stir in fruit and nuts. Combine honey, sugars and the water in small saucepan; stir over low heat until sugar dissolves. Simmer, uncovered, without stirring, 5 minutes. Pour hot syrup then chocolate into nut mixture; mix well.
3. Press mixture firmly into pan; press a 20cm (8-inch) round of baking paper on top.
4. Bake 40 minutes; cool in pan. Remove panforte from pan, discard baking paper; wrap in foil. Stand overnight before cutting into thin wedges to serve.

(PHOTOGRAPH PAGE 295)

JEWELLED Macaroons

PREP + COOK TIME 45 MINUTES (+ COOLING)   **MAKES** 24

1 egg white
¼ cup (55g) caster (superfine) sugar
¾ cup (60g) shredded coconut
2 tablespoons each finely chopped glacé apricot, glacé pineapple, glacé red cherries and glacé green cherries
2 tablespoons finely chopped roasted, unsalted pistachios

1. Preheat oven to 150°C/300°F. Line two 12-hole (1-tablespoon/20ml) mini muffin pans with paper cases.
2. Beat egg white in small bowl with electric mixer until soft peaks form; gradually add sugar, beating until sugar dissolves. Fold coconut and half the combined fruit and nuts into egg white mixture.
3. Divide mixture between paper cases. Sprinkle with remaining fruit and nut mixture.
4. Bake about 20 minutes; cool macaroons in pans.

Cover macaroons with foil halfway through baking time if fruit on top starts to brown. You need about 50g (1½ ounces) of each glacé fruit.

JEWELLED
Macaroons

BABY CHOCOLATE Christmas Cakes

PREP + COOK TIME 3 HOURS 20 MINUTES (+ STANDING & COOLING) MAKES 8

2⅓ cups (375g) sultanas
2⅓ cups (375g) coarsely chopped raisins
1½ cups (250g) dried currants
1½ cups (250g) seeded prunes, chopped coarsely
⅓ cup (55g) mixed peel
½ cup (100g) red glacé cherries, quartered
2 cups (500ml) tokay or port
2 cups (440g) firmly packed dark brown sugar
250g (8 ounces) butter, softened
6 eggs
¾ cup (90g) pecans, chopped coarsely
2 cups (300g) plain (all-purpose) flour
¾ cup (110g) self-raising flour
½ cup (50g) cocoa powder
250g (8 ounces) ready-made white icing

1. Combine fruit, 1½ cups of the tokay and ½ cup of the brown sugar in large bowl. Cover; stand overnight or for several days.
2. Preheat oven to 150°C/300°F. Line bases and sides of eight deep 10cm (4-inch) square cake pans with one layer each of brown paper and baking paper, extending paper 2cm (¾ inch) over sides.
3. Beat butter and remaining sugar in large bowl with electric mixer until combined. Beat in eggs, one at a time. Stir butter mixture into fruit mixture. Stir in nuts and sifted dry ingredients, in two batches. Divide mixture into pans; smooth tops.
4. Bake cakes about 1¾ hours. Brush hot cakes with remaining tokay. Cover cakes, in pans, tightly with foil; turn cakes upside down to cool overnight.
5. To decorate, roll icing between sheets of baking paper to 3mm (⅛-inch) thick; cut 1cm (½-inch) thick ribbons, attach to cake tops with a little water. Using 3cm (1¼-inch) star cutters, cut stars from icing. Brush back of stars with a little water; attach to top of ribbons. Stand for several hours or until dry. Wrap sides of cakes with a christmas ribbon.

TO STORE UN-ICED CAKES
Turn cakes out of pan, remove lining paper from side of cakes. Wrap tightly in plastic wrap. Place cakes in an airtight container to protect them. Store in the refrigerator for up to 3 months, or freeze for up to a year. Thaw frozen cakes in the refrigerator for 2 days.

Tokay is a sweet white fortified wine.
This recipe will also make one deep 20cm (8-inch) square or one deep 23cm (9-inch) round cake. Line pan with one layer of brown paper and two layers of baking paper. Bake about 3 hours.

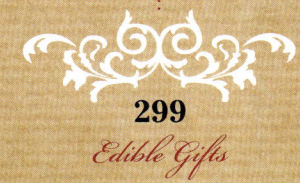

SPICED WREATH
Biscuits

(RECIPE PAGE 302)

MINCE PIES
(Three-in-One Fruit Mix)
(RECIPE PAGE 303)

SPICED WREATH Biscuits

125g (4 ounces) butter, softened
½ cup (110g) firmly packed light brown sugar
½ cup (125ml) treacle
1 egg, separated
2 cups (300g) plain (all-purpose) flour
½ cup (75g) self-raising flour
1 teaspoon bicarbonate of soda (baking soda)
2 teaspoons ground ginger
1 teaspoon ground cinnamon
¼ teaspoon ground cardamom
2 tablespoons raw sugar
⅓ cup (25g) flaked almonds

PREP + COOK TIME 1 HOUR (+ REFRIGERATION) MAKES 40

1. Preheat oven to 180°C/350°F. Line oven trays with baking paper.
2. Beat butter, brown sugar, treacle and egg yolk in small bowl with electric mixer until pale and creamy. Transfer to large bowl. Stir in sifted flours, soda and spices. Turn dough onto floured surface, knead until smooth. Cover with plastic wrap, refrigerate 30 minutes.
3. Divide dough into two portions; roll each portion separately on lightly floured surface until 4mm (⅛ inch) thick. Cut out rounds using 7cm (3-inch) fluted cutter. Use 3cm (1¼-inch) fluted cutter to cut an inner circle from each disc. Transfer to trays. Brush tops of dough with lightly beaten egg white; sprinkle half the biscuits with raw sugar and remaining biscuits with nuts. Bake about 10 minutes or until browned lightly. Stand 5 minutes, then transfer to wire racks to cool.

Store biscuits in an airtight container for up to 2 weeks.

(PHOTOGRAPH ALSO PAGE 300)

MINCE PIES
(Three-in-One Fruit Mix)

PREP + COOK TIME 1 HOUR (+ REFRIGERATION & STANDING)   MAKES 12

1 cup (150g) plain (all-purpose) flour
1 tablespoon icing (confectioners') sugar
1 tablespoon custard powder
90g (3 ounces) cold butter, chopped coarsely
1 egg, separated
1 tablespoon iced water, approximately
1 cup three-in-one fruit mix (page 197)
1 teaspoon finely grated lemon rind
1 tablespoon white (granulated) sugar

1. Grease 12-hole (2 tablespoon/40ml) round-based patty pan.
2. Process flour, icing sugar, custard powder and butter until crumbly. Add egg yolk and enough of the water to make ingredients come together. Knead dough on lightly floured surface until smooth. Cover with plastic wrap; refrigerate 30 minutes.
3. Preheat oven to 200°C/400°F.
4. Roll two-thirds of pastry between sheets of baking paper until 3mm (1/8-inch) thick. Cut 12 x 7.5cm (3-inch) rounds from pastry. Re-roll pastry scraps if necessary to make 12 rounds. Press rounds into tray, reserve pastry scraps.
5. Combine fruit mix and rind in medium bowl. Drop level tablespoons of mixture into pastry cases.
6. Roll reserved pastry until 3mm (1/8-inch) thick. Cut out 12 x 4.5cm (1¾-inch) stars with a cutter. Place stars on pies; brush with egg white, sprinkle with white sugar.
7. Bake pies about 20 minutes or until browned lightly. Stand pies in pan 5 minutes before transferring to wire rack to cool.

Store pies in an airtight container for a week, or freeze for up to 3 months; thaw pies overnight in the refrigerator.

(PHOTOGRAPH PAGE 301)

GLAZED FRUIT
Stollen

PREP + COOK TIME 1 HOUR 30 MINUTES (+ STANDING) **MAKES** 2 LOAVES (EACH LOAF MAKES 12 SLICES)

1¼ cups (310ml) warm milk
14g (½ ounce) dried yeast
½ cup (110g) caster (superfine) sugar
4¾ cups (700g) bread flour
¼ teaspoon sea salt
250g (8 ounces) butter, softened slightly
2 eggs
¾ cup (120g) sultanas
½ cup (80g) dried currants
½ cup (80g) finely chopped dried apricots
⅓ cup (55g) mixed peel
¼ cup (50g) red glacé cherries, quartered
⅓ cup (55g) slivered almonds, chopped coarsely
1 tablespoon finely grated lemon rind
250g (8 ounces) marzipan
1½ cups (240g) pure icing (confectioners') sugar
2 tablespoons milk, extra

1. Combine milk, yeast and 1 tablespoon of the caster sugar in small bowl; cover, stand in a warm place about 10 minutes or until mixture is frothy.
2. Meanwhile, sift flour, salt and remaining sugar into large bowl; rub in butter.
3. Stir yeast mixture and eggs into flour mixture; mix to a soft, sticky dough. Stir in fruit, nuts and rind. Place dough in oiled bowl, cover with oiled plastic wrap; stand in warm place about 1 hour or until doubled in size.
4. Grease two oven trays.
5. Turn dough onto floured surface, knead about 5 minutes or until smooth. Divide dough in half. Roll each half into 20cm x 30cm (8-inch x 12-inch) rectangle. Roll marzipan into two 25cm (10-inch) logs; place along centre of dough. Fold dough over marzipan, transfer to trays. Cover with oiled plastic wrap, stand in warm place about 1 hour or until doubled in size.
6. Preheat oven to 200°C/400°F.
7. Bake stollen 15 minutes. Reduce oven to 160°C/325°F. Bake a further 25 minutes or until browned and hollow sounding when tapped. Stand on trays 5 minutes before transferring to wire racks to cool.
8. Sift icing sugar into medium bowl; stir in extra milk. Drizzle glaze over warm stollen.

Bread flour is a strong flour, meaning that it has a relatively high gluten (protein) content; this causes the bread to rise, giving it shape and structure. It is available from most supermarkets. Stollen will keep in an airtight container for up to a month. It's delicious toasted lightly under the grill (broiler); serve buttered.

CINNAMON
and Sour Cherry Macaroons

PREP + COOK TIME 1 HOUR 15 MINUTES (+ REFRIGERATION, STANDING & COOLING) **MAKES** 20

3 egg whites
¼ cup (55g) caster (superfine) sugar
1¼ cups (200g) icing (confectioners') sugar
1 cup (120g) ground almonds
½ teaspoon ground cinnamon

SOUR CHERRY CURD
½ cup (100g) drained seeded morello sour cherries
3 egg yolks
⅓ cup (55g) caster (superfine) sugar
1 tablespoon lemon juice
2 teaspoons kirsch
60g (2 ounces) unsalted butter, chopped coarsely

CINNAMON SUGAR
2 tablespoons icing (confectioners') sugar
½ teaspoon ground cinnamon

1. Make sour cherry curd and cinnamon sugar.
2. Grease oven trays; line with baking paper.
3. Beat egg whites in small bowl with electric mixer until soft peaks form. Add caster sugar, beat until sugar is dissolved. Transfer mixture to large bowl. Fold in sifted icing sugar, ground almonds and cinnamon, in two batches.
4. Spoon mixture into piping bag fitted with 2cm (¾-inch) plain tube. Pipe 4cm (1½-inch) rounds about 2cm (¾-inch) apart on trays. Tap trays on bench so macaroons spread slightly. Dust macaroons with half the sifted cinnamon sugar; stand about 30 minutes or until dry to touch.
5. Meanwhile, preheat oven to 150°C/300°F.
6. Bake macaroons about 20 minutes; cool on trays.
7. Sandwich macaroons with sour cherry curd; dust with remaining sifted cinnamon sugar.

SOUR CHERRY CURD
Blend or process cherries until smooth; you will need 2 tablespoons puree for this recipe. Place egg yolks and sugar in medium heatproof bowl over medium saucepan of simmering water; whisk until thick and sugar is dissolved. Whisk in cherry puree, juice and kirsch. Add butter; whisk about 5 minutes or until mixture is thick and holds the trail of the whisk. Refrigerate until firm.

CINNAMON SUGAR
Combine ingredients in small bowl.

Unfilled macaroons will keep in an airtight container for about a week. Filled macaroons will keep in an airtight container in the refrigerator for up to 2 days.

CHAPTER 8
BOXING *Day*

JINGLE BELLS
Jingle Bells

ADD A SPLASH OF COLOUR
to your hallway with a bell jar
filled with colourful Christmas baubles.
For this you will need a bell jar or **GLASS CAKE STAND**
with a dome lid, lots of
CHRISTMAS BAUBLES of any colour, a plate a little larger than the dome
(unless using a cake stand) and a helping hand.
One person will need to hold **THE BELL JAR**
or dome upside down while it is filled as full as possible with **BAUBLES**.
GIVE THE JAR A GOOD SHAKE to close up any gaps.
Place a plate over the hole and carefully return the
JAR OR DOME the right way up to create
a colourful domed
decoration.

Panettone is the traditional Italian Christmas 'cake' served on Christmas Day. It's a light, sweet bread containing candied citrus peel – variations can also include sultanas or raisins and sometimes even chocolate. Slices of leftover panettone make delicious French toast, perfect for a lazy Boxing Day breakfast.

PANETTONE TOAST
with Peaches and Blueberries

PREP + COOK TIME 15 MINUTES SERVES 4

1 cup (500ml) milk
2 eggs
2 tablespoons caster (superfine) sugar
8 thick slices panettone (450g)
cooking-oil spray
⅔ cup (190g) vanilla yogurt
2 yellow peaches (340g), cut into wedges
⅔ cup (100g) fresh blueberries
2 teaspoons icing (confectioners') sugar

1 Whisk milk, eggs and caster sugar in shallow bowl until combined. Add panettone slices, one at a time, turning to coat and soak 30 seconds.
2 Coat base of large frying pan with oil spray. Lift panettone slices from egg mixture with slotted spoon, drain; cook slices about 1 minute each side or until puffed and golden.
3 Top toast with yogurt and fruit; dust with sifted icing sugar.

Serve with ice-cream instead of yogurt for a quick dessert. If possible, choose freestone peaches (or nectarines) rather than the clingstone variety. You can use any seasonal fruit for this recipe.

CHICKEN Fried Rice

PREP + COOK TIME 15 MINUTES SERVES 4

Stir-fry 5 cups cooked long-grain white rice with 1 cup frozen peas, 1 cup corn kernels, 3 cups shredded cooked chicken, 6 sliced green onions (scallions), 1 finely chopped red capsicum (bell pepper) and ⅓ cup light soy sauce; toss until heated through. Season to taste. Chicken fried rice tastes wonderful cold.

CHICKEN Pasta Salad

PREPARATION TIME 15 MINUTES SERVES 4

Combine 4 cups cooked penne pasta with 150g (4½ ounces) crumbled fetta cheese, 150g (4½ ounces) chopped char-grilled red capsicum (bell pepper), 3 cups chopped cooked chicken, ⅓ cup roasted chopped walnuts, 1 cup loosely packed fresh basil leaves and ½ cup italian dressing in large bowl. Season to taste.

CHICKEN Caesar Salad

PREP TIME 15 MINUTES SERVES 4

Toss together 1 sliced cos lettuce, 6 slices chopped cooked crisp bacon, 3 cups shredded cooked chicken, 4 quartered hard-boiled eggs, ½ cup flaked parmesan cheese and ½ cup caesar salad dressing in large bowl. Season to taste.

CHICKEN Wraps

PREP TIME 10 MINUTES MAKES 8

Top 8 tortillas with 1 chopped tomato, 1 sliced avocado, ½ small chopped red onion, 3 cups shredded cooked chicken, 1 cup loosely packed fresh coriander (cilantro) sprigs and ⅔ cup chunky salsa; season to taste. Roll tortillas to enclose filling.

TURKEY COTTAGE *Loaf*

TURKEY COTTAGE *Loaf*

PREP + COOK TIME 30 MINUTES SERVES 8

6 medium zucchini (720g), sliced thinly lengthways
1 cup (240g) ricotta cheese
¼ cup finely chopped fresh flat-leaf parsley
2 tablespoons finely chopped fresh mint
1 clove garlic, crushed
1 round cob loaf (450g)
½ cup (150g) chunky rocket (arugula) and cashew dip
300g (9½ ounces) thinly sliced cooked turkey

1 Barbecue or grill zucchini until tender; cool.
2 Combine cheese, herbs and garlic in medium bowl; season.
3 Cut shallow lid from top of loaf; remove soft bread from inside loaf, leaving 2cm (¾-inch) thick shell.
4 Spread dip all over the inside of the bread shell and lid. Layer zucchini, turkey and ricotta mixture three or four times inside bread shell. Press mixture down firmly; replace lid, pressing down firmly.
5 Tie loaf tightly with kitchen string then enclose in plastic wrap. Refrigerate loaf about 2 hours or until ready to serve.

You can buy char-grilled zucchini from the deli section at most supermarkets; you will need about 2½ cups.

PORK SALAD WITH *Chilli Plum Dressing*

PREP TIME 20 MINUTES SERVES 4

1 medium wombok (napa cabbage) (1kg), shredded finely
½ cup finely shredded fresh mint
1 small red onion (100g), sliced thinly
400g (12½ ounces) leftover roast pork, shredded finely
½ cup firmly packed fresh mint leaves
CHILLI PLUM DRESSING
½ cup (150g) mayonnaise
½ cup (125ml) plum sauce
1 teaspoon dried chilli flakes
2 tablespoons water

1 Make chilli plum dressing.
2 Place wombok, shredded mint, onion and half the pork in large bowl with half the dressing; toss gently to combine.
3 Divide wombok mixture among serving plates; top with remaining pork and the mint leaves, drizzle with remaining dressing.

CHILLI PLUM DRESSING
Whisk ingredients in small bowl; season to taste.

(PHOTOGRAPH PAGE 318)

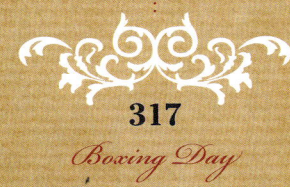

PORK SALAD WITH
Chilli Plum Dressing
(RECIPE PAGE 317)

HAM, EGG AND CHEESE
Toasties

PREP + COOK TIME 10 MINUTES **MAKES** 1

Preheat sandwich press. Sandwich sliced ham, thinly sliced hard-boiled egg and coarsely grated cheddar cheese between 2 slices wholemeal bread; season. Toast in sandwich press. Serve with barbecue sauce, if you like.

TURKEY AND TOMATO
Salsa Quesadillas

PREP + COOK TIME 15 MINUTES **MAKES** 4

Preheat sandwich press. Place 4 tortillas on cutting board. Sprinkle with coarsely grated tasty cheese; top with sliced cooked turkey, spicy tomato salsa then more cheese. Season. Top with 4 tortillas. Toast in sandwich press.

TURKEY ON TOASTED
Turkish

PREP + COOK TIME 10 MINUTES **MAKES** 1

Preheat sandwich press. Split 1 small turkish bread roll in half. Spread cut sides with cranberry sauce then sandwich sliced turkey, shaved jarlsberg (swiss) cheese and baby spinach leaves between pieces; season. Toast in sandwich press.

ITALIAN-STYLE TOASTED
Buns

PREP + COOK TIME 10 MINUTES **MAKES** 4

Preheat sandwich press. Split 4 buns in half; spread bases with chunky basil pesto. Top with sliced ham, sliced mozzarella cheese, sliced artichoke hearts, char-grilled capsicum (bell pepper) and a handful of rocket (arugula); season, top with bun tops. Toast in sandwich press.

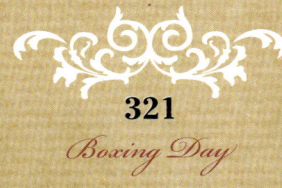

RICOTTA ZUCCHINI
and Ham Wrap

PREP TIME 10 MINUTES SERVES 2

Slice 2 small zucchini lengthways into ribbons using a vegetable peeler. Spread 3 rye mountain bread wraps with ricotta cheese; top with zucchini and sliced ham. Season; roll to enclose. Cut to serve.

NEW YORK-STYLE
Deli Sandwich

PREP TIME 5 MINUTES MAKES 4

Spread 8 slices sourdough with dijon mustard; top 4 sourdough slices with drained sauerkraut, sliced ham and sliced swiss cheese. Season; top with remaining sourdough slices.

ROAST BEEF
and Coleslaw on Rye

PREP TIME 10 MINUTES SERVES 2

Spread 2 slices rye bread with horseradish cream; top with sliced rare roast beef and coleslaw. Season; top with another 2 slices rye bread.

TURKEY AND SALAD
Pocket

PREP TIME 15 MINUTES SERVES 4

Coarsely shred about 2 large cos lettuce leaves. Combine leaves in large bowl with coarsely chopped cooked turkey, finely chopped celery, diced lebanese cucumber, finely sliced radishes, mayonnaise and lemon juice; season to taste. Make a slit in 4 baby pitta pockets; line each pocket with a cos lettuce leaf. Spoon turkey mixture into pockets.

TURKEY CRANBERRY
and Peanut Salad

TURKEY CRANBERRY
and Peanut Salad

PREP TIME 20 MINUTES   SERVES 6

1kg (2 pounds) cooked turkey breast
½ cup (125ml) red wine vinegar
1 teaspoon dijon mustard
¼ cup (60ml) light olive oil
⅔ cup (90g) dried cranberries
3 stalks celery (450g), trimmed, sliced thinly
1¼ cups (100g) bean sprouts
1 cup (50g) snow pea sprouts
½ cup (70g) roasted unsalted peanuts
½ cup firmly packed fresh mint leaves, torn
1 butter (boston) lettuce, leaves separated

1 Coarsely shred turkey.
2 Combine vinegar, mustard and oil in large bowl. Add turkey, cranberries, celery, sprouts, nuts and mint; toss gently to combine. Season to taste.
3 Serve salad on lettuce leaves.

You can also make this salad with leftover barbecued chicken.
If taking this salad on a picnic, pack salad ingredients and dressing separately and assemble on location.

HAM ZUCCHINI
and Fetta Loaves

PREP + COOK TIME 45 MINUTES   MAKES 8

1 cup (150g) self-raising flour
5 eggs
¼ cup (60ml) olive oil
70g (2½ ounces) fetta cheese, crumbled
½ cup (60g) coarsely grated cheddar cheese
2 large slices ham (150g), chopped finely
1 medium brown onion (150g), chopped finely
3 medium zucchini (360g), grated coarsely
¼ cup each finely chopped fresh mint and flat-leaf parsley
8 baby grape tomatoes, halved

1 Preheat oven to 200°C/400°F.
2 Grease eight-hole (¾-cup/180ml) petite loaf pan; line each hole with a strip of baking paper, extending paper over short sides.
3 Sift flour into large bowl; whisk in eggs and oil. Stir in cheeses, ham, vegetables and herbs; season. Spoon mixture into pan holes; top with tomato halves.
4 Bake loaves about 30 minutes. Stand loaves in pan 5 minutes; turn onto wire rack to cool.

You can also bake this mixture in one loaf pan; it will take about 45 minutes to cook.
Loaves are best made on the day of serving.

(PHOTOGRAPH PAGE 326)

HAM, ZUCCHINI
and Fetta Loaves
(RECIPE PAGE 325)

TOMATO FETTA
and Ham Frittatas

(RECIPE PAGE 328)

TOMATO FETTA
and Ham Frittatas

PREP + COOK TIME 35 MINUTES MAKES 6

100g (3 ounces) coarsely chopped sliced ham
100g (3 ounces) fetta cheese
¼ cup (20g) finely grated parmesan cheese
⅓ cup coarsely chopped fresh basil
6 eggs
⅔ cup (160ml) pouring cream
9 cherry tomatoes, halved

1. Preheat oven to 180°C/350°F. Line holes of six-hole (¾-cup/180ml) texas muffin pan with squares of baking paper.
2. Divide ham, cheeses and basil into pan holes.
3. Whisk eggs and cream in medium bowl, season; pour into pan holes. Top each frittata with three cherry tomato halves.
4. Bake frittatas about 25 minutes. Stand frittatas in pan 5 minutes before turning out.

These frittatas are delicious served warm or cold, making them perfect to take on a picnic.

(PHOTOGRAPH PAGE 327)

FRUIT CAKE
Cream Parfaits

PREP TIME 20 MINUTES SERVES 6

250g (8 ounces) mascarpone cheese
¼ cup (60ml) whisky
1 tablespoon icing (confectioners') sugar
½ cup (125ml) thickened (heavy) cream, whipped
300g (4½ ounces) fruit cake, crumbled

1. Combine mascarpone, 2 tablespoons of the whisky and sifted icing sugar in large bowl; fold in cream.
2. Sprinkle half the cake into six ¾-cup (180ml) glasses; sprinkle with half the remaining whisky. Spoon in half the mascarpone mixture. Repeat layering with remaining cake, whisky and mascarpone mixture. Cover; refrigerate until required. Serve topped with fresh raspberries and sifted icing sugar, if you like.

FRUIT CAKE
Cream Parfaits

FRUIT CAKE
Ice-cream Terrine

PREP TIME *15 MINUTES (+ FREEZING)* **SERVES 6**

450g (14½ ounces) fruit cake, cut into 1.5cm (¾-inch) slices
2 tablespoons orange-flavoured liqueur
2 litres (8 cups) vanilla ice-cream, softened
1 tablespoon finely grated orange rind

1. Line 14cm x 21cm (5½-inch x 8½-inch) loaf pan with plastic wrap.
2. Brush cake slices with liqueur.
3. Place ice-cream in large bowl; stir in rind.
4. Spread half the ice-cream mixture into pan; top with cake slices then remaining ice-cream. Cover with plastic wrap; freeze until firm. Using hot knife, cut terrine into six slices.

Serve with fresh mixed berries.

FRUIT CAKE
and Eggnog Cheesecake
(RECIPE PAGE 334)

FRUIT CAKE
and Eggnog Cheesecake

LEFTOVER FRUIT CAKE provides the base for this baked cheesecake. The rich, creamy filling **CONTAINS BRANDY** (or you could use lemon juice) and the whole thing is topped with fresh fruit covered in a **WEB OF TOFFEE**. It's a wonderful dessert, perfect for **BOXING DAY** when there's bound to be some leftover cake, but so delicious you'll probably want to make it more often than that. **BOUGHT FRUIT CAKE** can be used instead of your own rich **CHRISTMAS CAKE,** but of course it won't be as good. You can also make this cheesecake in a rectangular cake pan and **CUT IT INTO SQUARES.** Place the little squares in boxes lined with baking paper. **TIE THE BOXES** with red or white ribbon and decorate with **FRESH HOLLY** or whatever vibrant **GREEN FOLIAGE** you can find. Give them to friends as a late *Christmas present.*

FRUIT CAKE
and Eggnog Cheesecake

PREP + COOK TIME 1 HOUR 15 MINUTES (+ COOLING & REFRIGERATION) SERVES 10

350g (11 ounces) fruit cake, cut into 1cm (½-inch) slices
750g (1½ pounds) cream cheese, softened
300g (9½ ounces) sour cream
1 teaspoon vanilla extract
¼ cup (60ml) brandy
½ teaspoon ground nutmeg
2 cups (440g) caster (superfine) sugar
3 eggs
1 cup (250ml) water
1 medium pink grapefruit (425g), segmented
1 large orange (300g), segmented
150g (4½ ounces) strawberries, sliced thinly
100g (3 ounces) red seedless grapes, sliced thinly
1 large kiwifruit (100g), sliced thinly

1. Preheat oven to 180°C/350°F. Line base of 22cm (9-inch) springform tin with baking paper.
2. Cover base of tin with cake slices, trimming to fit. Bake about 10 minutes or until browned lightly.
3. Reduce oven to 150°C/300°F.
4. Meanwhile, beat cream cheese, sour cream, extract, brandy, nutmeg and half the sugar in medium bowl with electric mixer until smooth. Beat in eggs, one at a time. Pour mixture into tin.
5. Bake cheesecake about 45 minutes or until just set. Cool cheesecake in oven with door ajar. Cover; refrigerate overnight.
6. Stir remaining sugar and the water in medium heavy-based frying pan over high heat until sugar dissolves; bring to the boil. Reduce heat; simmer, without stirring, uncovered, about 10 minutes or until toffee mixture is golden brown in colour. Remove from heat; stand until bubbles subside.
7. Meanwhile, remove cheesecake from tin, place on serving plate; top with fruit. Working quickly, drizzle toffee over fruit.

(PHOTOGRAPH ALSO PAGE 332)

LITTLE CHOCOLATE
Christmas Puddings

PREP + COOK TIME 45 MINUTES (+ REFRIGERATION & STANDING)   MAKES 44

700g (1½ pounds) christmas pudding
250g (8 ounces) dark eating (semi-sweet) chocolate, melted
½ cup (125ml) brandy
½ cup (80g) icing (confectioners') sugar
200g (6½ ounces) white chocolate melts
red and green glacé cherries, cut to resemble berries and leaves

1. Crumble pudding into large bowl. Stir in melted chocolate, brandy and sifted icing sugar; mix well.
2. Roll level tablespoons of mixture into balls, place on tray; cover, refrigerate until firm.
3. Melt white chocolate in small heatproof bowl over small saucepan of simmering water. Cool chocolate 10 minutes.
4. Drizzle chocolate over puddings to form "custard"; decorate with cherries. Stand at room temperature until set.

Use either bought or leftover homemade pudding for this recipe.
This recipe can be made 2 weeks ahead.
If the weather is hot or humid you may need to store puddings in the refrigerator.

CHRISTMAS ICE-CREAM
Pudding Bites

PREP + COOK TIME 20 MINUTES (+ FREEZING) MAKES 28

2 cups (400ml) vanilla ice-cream, softened
200g (6½ ounces) christmas pudding, chopped finely
400g (12½ ounces) dark eating (semi-sweet) chocolate, chopped coarsely

1. Grease two 14-hole ice-cube trays. Line small oven tray with baking paper. Place 28 mini muffin paper cases on another small tray.
2. Working quickly, combine ice-cream and pudding in medium bowl; press mixture into ice-cube tray holes. Freeze about 2 hours or until firm. Unmould bites onto tray; freeze 30 minutes.
3. Meanwhile, melt half the chocolate in medium heatproof bowl over medium saucepan of simmering water. Remove from heat; stand 5 minutes.
4. Working quickly and using small cocktail toothpicks, dip half the ice-cream blocks, one at a time, into chocolate until covered; place on baking-paper-lined tray. Freeze until ready to serve.
5. Repeat melting and dipping with remaining chocolate and ice-cream blocks; freeze until ready to serve. Serve bites in paper cases.

These little morsels only improve with time. Make 1 or 2 days ahead.
Use rounded ice-cube trays if possible as the ice-cream blocks will unmould more easily. You can also make this as a log. Place ice-cream mixture in a bar cake pan lined with baking paper. Once frozen, place on a wire rack and drizzle with melted chocolate to cover. Transfer to a serving plate; freeze until ready to serve.

GLOSSARY

ALLSPICE also called pimento or jamaican pepper; tastes of nutmeg, cumin, clove and cinnamon. Available whole or ground.

BAKING PAPER also called parchment paper or baking parchment; is a silicone-coated paper that is primarily used for lining baking pans and oven trays so cakes and biscuits won't stick, making removal easy.

BAKING POWDER a raising agent consisting mainly of two parts cream of tartar to one part bicarbonate of soda.

BAY LEAVES aromatic leaves from the bay tree available fresh or dried; adds a peppery flavour.

BEANS
borlotti also called roman beans or pink beans, can be eaten fresh or dried. Interchangeable with pinto beans due to their similarity in appearance – pale pink or beige with dark-red streaks.
broad (fava) also called windsor and horse beans; available dried, fresh, canned and frozen. Fresh should be peeled twice (discarding both the outer long green pod and the beige-green tough inner shell); frozen beans have had their pods removed but the beige shell still needs to be removed.

BEETROOT (BEETS) also called red beets; a firm, round root vegetable.

BETEL LEAVES are large tender green leaves grown in tropical areas and sometimes called piper leaves. They are commonly used to make snacks in Thailand, Burma, India and Sri Lanka. Torn leaves may also be added to curries. They are available from Asian supermarkets and some greengrocers. If unavailable use large baby spinach leaves.

BICARBONATE OF SODA also known as baking soda.

BREAD
brioche French in origin; a rich, yeast-leavened, cake-like bread made with butter and eggs. Available from cake or specialty bread shops.
ciabatta in Italian, the word means slipper, the traditional shape of this popular crisp-crusted, open-textured white sourdough bread. A good bread to use for bruschetta.

BURGHUL also called bulghur wheat; hulled steamed wheat kernels that, once dried, are crushed into various-sized grains. Used in Middle-Eastern dishes such as felafel, kibbeh and tabbouleh. Is not the same as cracked wheat.

BUTTER we use salted butter unless stated otherwise; 125g is equal to 1 stick (4 ounces).

BUTTERMILK originally the term given to the slightly sour liquid left after butter was churned from cream, today it is made from no-fat or low-fat milk to which specific bacterial cultures have been added. Despite its name, it is actually low in fat.

CAPERS the grey-green buds of a warm climate shrub, sold either dried and salted or pickled in a vinegar brine; tiny young ones, called baby capers, are available in brine or dried in salt.

CAPSICUM (BELL PEPPER) also called pepper; discard seeds and membranes before use.

CARAWAY SEEDS the small, half-moon-shaped dried seed from a member of the parsley family; adds a sharp anise flavour when used in both sweet and savoury dishes.

CARDAMOM a spice native to India and used extensively in its cuisine; can be purchased in pod, seed or ground form.

CHEESE
blue mould-treated cheeses mottled with blue veining.
bocconcini from the diminutive of "boccone", meaning mouthful in Italian; walnut-sized, baby mozzarella. A delicate, semi-soft, white cheese traditionally made from buffalo milk. Sold fresh, it spoils rapidly so will only keep, refrigerated in brine, 1 or 2 days at the most.
brie soft-ripened cow's-milk cheese with a delicate, creamy texture and a rich, sweet taste that varies from buttery to mushroomy. Best served at room temperature. After a brief period of ageing, brie should have a bloomy white rind and creamy, voluptuous centre, which becomes runny with ripening.
fetta Greek in origin; a crumbly textured goat's- or sheep-milk cheese with a sharp, salty taste. Ripened and stored in salted whey.
goat's made from goat's milk, has an earthy, strong taste. Available in soft, crumbly and firm textures, in various shapes and sizes, and sometimes rolled in ash or herbs.
haloumi a Greek Cypriot cheese with a semi-firm, spongy texture and very salty sweet flavour. Ripened and stored in salted whey; best grilled or fried, and holds its shape well on being heated. Eat while still warm as it becomes tough and rubbery on cooling.
mascarpone an Italian fresh cultured-cream product made in much the same way as yogurt. Whiteish to creamy yellow in colour, with a soft, creamy buttery-rich, luscious texture.
parmesan also called parmigiano; is a hard, grainy cow's-milk cheese originating in Italy. Reggiano is the best variety.
pecorino the generic Italian name for cheeses made from sheep milk. This family of hard, white to pale-yellow cheeses, traditionally made in the Italian winter and spring when sheep graze on natural pastures, has been matured for 8 to 12 months. If you can't find it, use parmesan cheese.
ricotta a soft, sweet, moist, white cow's-milk cheese with a low fat content (8.5%) and a slightly grainy texture. The name roughly translates as "cooked again" and refers to ricotta's manufacture from a whey that is itself a by-product of other cheese making.

CHERVIL also known as cicily; mildly fennel-flavoured member of the parsley family with curly dark-green leaves. Available both fresh and dried but, like all herbs, is best used fresh; like coriander and parsley, its delicate flavour diminishes the longer it's cooked.

CHICKEN, TENDERLOIN thin strip of meat lying just under the breast; good for stir-frying.

CHICKPEAS (GARBANZO BEANS) also called hummus or channa; an irregularly round, sandy-coloured legume used in Mediterranean, Indian and Hispanic cooking. Has a firm texture, even after cooking, a floury mouth-feel and a robust nutty flavour; available canned or dried (reconstitute for several hours in cold water before use).

CHILLI use rubber gloves when handling fresh chillies as they can burn your skin. We use unseeded chillies because the seeds contain the heat; use fewer chillies rather than seed the lot.
cayenne pepper a long, extremely hot, dried, ground red chilli native to South America.
chipotle pronounced cheh-pot-lay. A dried and smoked jalapeño chilli with a deep, intensely smoky flavour; the chipotle is dark brown in colour and wrinkled in appearance.
jalapeño pronounced hah-lah-pen-yo. Fairly hot, medium-sized, plump, dark-green chilli; available pickled, canned or bottled, and fresh.
red thai (serrano) also called scuds or bird's eye chillies; tiny, very hot and bright red.

CHINESE COOKING WINE also called shao hsing or chinese rice wine; made from fermented rice, wheat and sugar. Substitute mirin or sherry.

CHOCOLATE
dark eating (semi-sweet) also known as luxury chocolate; made of a high percentage of cocoa liquor and cocoa butter, and little added sugar. Unless stated otherwise, we use dark eating chocolate in this book as it's ideal for use in desserts and cakes.
melts small discs of compounded milk, white or dark chocolate ideal for melting and moulding.
white eating contains no cocoa solids but derives its sweet flavour from cocoa butter. Very sensitive to heat.

CHORIZO sausage of Spanish origin, made of coarsely ground pork and highly seasoned with garlic and chilli. They are deeply smoked, very spicy and dry-cured so that they do not need cooking.

CINNAMON available in pieces (called sticks or quills) and ground into powder; one of the world's most common spices.

CLOVES dried flower buds of a tropical tree; can be used whole or ground; has a strong scent and taste so use sparingly.

COCOA POWDER also known as unsweetened cocoa; cocoa beans (cacao seeds) that have been fermented, roasted, shelled and ground into powder then cleared of most of the fat content.

COCONUT, DESICCATED concentrated, dried, unsweetened and finely shredded coconut flesh.

CORIANDER (CILANTRO) also called pak chee or chinese parsley; bright-green-leafed herb with both pungent aroma and taste. Both the stems and roots of coriander are used in Thai cooking: wash well before chopping. Coriander seeds are dried and sold either whole or ground, and neither form tastes remotely like the fresh leaf.

CORNFLOUR (CORNSTARCH) available made from corn or wheat; used as a thickening agent in cooking.

CRANBERRIES available dried and frozen; have a rich, astringent flavour and can be used in cooking sweet and savoury dishes. The dried version can usually be substituted for or with other dried fruit.

CREAM
pouring also called fresh cream or pure cream. It has no additives, unlike thickened cream. Minimum fat content 35%.
thickened (heavy) a whipping cream containing a thickener. Minimum fat content 35%.

CREAM OF TARTAR the acid ingredient in baking powder; added to confectionery mixtures to help prevent sugar from crystallising. Keeps frostings creamy and improves volume when beating egg whites.

CREME FRAICHE a mature, naturally fermented cream with a velvety texture and slightly tangy, nutty flavour. Minimum fat content 35%. A French variation of sour cream, it boils without curdling and can be used in sweet and savoury dishes.

CUMIN also called zeera or comino; resembling caraway in size, cumin is the dried seed of a plant related to the parsley family. Its spicy, almost curry-like flavour is essential to the traditional foods of Mexico, India, North Africa and the Middle East. Available dried as seeds or ground.

CUSTARD POWDER instant mixture used to make pouring custard; it is similar to North American instant pudding mixes.

DAIKON also called white radish; this long, white horseradish has a wonderful, sweet flavour. After peeling, eat it raw in salads or shredded as a garnish; also great sliced or cubed and cooked in stir-fries. The flesh is white but the skin can be either white or black; buy those that are firm and unwrinkled from Asian food shops.

341
Glossary

EGGPLANT also called aubergine. Ranging in size from tiny to very large and in colour from pale green to deep purple. Can also be purchased char-grilled, packed in oil, in jars.

EGGS we use large chicken eggs weighing an average of 60g unless stated otherwise. If a recipe calls for raw or barely cooked eggs, exercise caution if there is a salmonella problem in your area, particularly in food eaten by children and pregnant women.

FENNEL also called finocchio or anise; a crunchy green vegetable slightly resembling celery that's eaten raw in salads; fried as an accompaniment; or used as an ingredient in soups and sauces. Also the name given to the dried seeds of the plant, which have a stronger licorice flavour.

FISH SAUCE called naam pla if Thai-made, nuoc naam if Vietnamese; the two are almost identical. Made from pulverised salted fermented fish (most often anchovies); has a pungent smell and strong taste. Available in varying degrees of intensity, use according to your taste.

FLOUR
plain (all-purpose) unbleached wheat flour; is the best for baking as the gluten content ensures a strong dough for a light result.
rice very fine, almost powdery, gluten-free flour made from ground white rice.
self-raising (self-rising) plain flour sifted with added baking powder in the proportion of 1 cup flour to 2 teaspoons baking powder..
wholemeal also known as wholewheat flour; milled with the wheat germ so is higher in fibre and more nutritional than plain flour.

GELATINE we use dried (powdered) gelatine in this book; it's also available in sheet form known as leaf gelatine. Three teaspoons of dried gelatine (8g or one sachet) is about the same as four gelatine leaves. The two types are interchangeable but leaf gelatine gives a much clearer mixture than dried gelatine.

GINGER
fresh also called green or root ginger; the thick gnarled root of a tropical plant. Can be kept, peeled, covered with dry sherry in a jar and refrigerated, or frozen in an airtight container.
glacé fresh ginger root preserved in sugar syrup; crystallised ginger can be used if rinsed with warm water and dried before using.
ground also called powdered ginger; used as a flavouring in baking but cannot be substituted for fresh ginger.

GLACE CHERRIES also called candied cherries; boiled in a heavy sugar syrup and then dried.

GLACE FRUIT fruit such as peaches, pineapple and orange cooked in a heavy sugar syrup then dried.

GLUCOSE SYRUP also known as liquid glucose, made from wheat starch. Available at most supermarkets.

GOLDEN SYRUP a by-product of refined sugarcane; pure maple syrup or honey can be substituted. Treacle is a similar product, however, it is more viscous and has a stronger flavour and aroma than golden syrup (which has been refined further and contains fewer impurities, so is lighter in colour and more fluid).

HORSERADISH commonly purchased in bottles at the supermarket in two forms: horseradish cream and prepared horseradish. These cannot be substituted one for the other in cooking but both can be used as table condiments.
cream commercially prepared creamy paste consisiting of grated horseradish, vinegar, oil and sugar.
prepared preserved grated horseradish.

KAFFIR LIME LEAVES also known as bai magrood and looks like two glossy dark-green leaves joined end to end, forming a rounded hourglass shape. Used fresh or dried in many South-East Asian dishes, they are used like bay leaves or curry leaves. Sold fresh, dried or frozen, the dried leaves are less potent so double the number if using them as a substitute for fresh; a strip of fresh lime peel may be substituted for each kaffir lime leaf.

KECAP MANIS a dark, thick, sweet soy sauce used in most South-East Asian cuisines.

KITCHEN STRING made of a natural product, so it neither affects the flavour of the food it's tied around nor melts when heated.

KUMARA the Polynesian name of an orange-fleshed sweet potato often confused with yam; good baked, boiled, mashed or fried similarly to other potatoes.

LYCHEES a small fruit from China with a hard shell and sweet, juicy flesh. The white flesh has a gelatinous texture and musky, perfumed taste. Discard the rough skin and seed before using in salads or as a dessert fruit. Also available canned in a sugar syrup.

MAPLE SYRUP (PURE) distilled from the sap of sugar maple trees. Maple-flavoured syrup or pancake syrup is not an adequate substitute for the real thing.

MARZIPAN made from ground almonds, sugar and glucose. Similar to almond paste, however, is not as strong in flavour, has a finer consistency and is more pliable. Cheaper brands often use ground apricot kernels and sugar.

MIRIN a Japanese champagne-coloured cooking wine, made of glutinous rice and alcohol. It is used expressly for cooking and should not be confused with sake.

MIXED PEEL candied citrus peel.

MIXED SPICE a classic spice mixture generally containing caraway, allspice, coriander, cumin, nutmeg and ginger, although cinnamon and other spices can be added. It is used with fruit and in cakes.

MORELLO SOUR CHERRIES bitter cherries available bottled in syrup. Used in baking and savoury dishes and a good match for game.

MUSHROOMS
button small, cultivated white mushrooms with a mild flavour. When a recipe in this book calls for an unspecified mushroom, use button.
enoki cultivated mushrooms also called enokitake; are tiny long-stemmed, pale mushrooms that grow and are sold in clusters, and can be used that way or separated by slicing off the base. They have a mild fruity flavour and are slightly crisp in texture.

shiitake, fresh also called chinese black, forest or golden oak mushrooms. Although cultivated, they have the earthiness and taste of wild mushrooms. They are large and meaty.
swiss brown also called roman or cremini. Light to dark brown mushrooms with full-bodied flavour; suited for use in casseroles or being stuffed and baked.

MUSTARD
dijon also called french. Pale brown, creamy, distinctively flavoured, fairly mild french mustard.
wholegrain also known as seeded. A French-style coarse-grain mustard made from crushed mustard seeds and dijon-style french mustard. Works well with cold meats and sausages.

NIGELLA SEEDS also called kalonji or black onion seeds. Tiny, angular seeds, black on the outside and creamy within, with a sharp nutty flavour that is enhanced by frying briefly in a dry hot pan before use. Can be found in most Middle-Eastern and Asian food shops. Sometimes erroneously called black cumin seeds.

NORI a type of dried seaweed used in Japanese cooking as a garnish, flavouring or for sushi. Sold in thin sheets, plain or toasted (yaki-nori).

NUTMEG a strong and pungent spice ground from the dried nut of an evergreen tree native to Indonesia. Usually found ground but the flavour is more intense from a whole nut, available from spice shops, so it's best to grate your own.

OIL
cooking spray we use a cholesterol-free spray made from canola oil.
olive made from ripened olives. Extra virgin and virgin are the first and second press, respectively, of the olives and are therefore considered the best; the "extra light" or "light" name on other types refers to taste not fat levels.
peanut pressed from ground peanuts; the most commonly used oil in Asian cooking because of its high smoke point (capacity to handle high heat without burning).
sesame made from roasted, crushed, white sesame seeds; a flavouring rather than a cooking medium.
vegetable any of a number of oils from plant rather than animal fats.

ONION
green (scallions) also called (incorrectly) shallot; an immature onion picked before the bulb has formed, having a long, bright-green edible stalk.
pickling also known as cocktail onions; are baby brown onions, larger than shallots.
red also known as spanish, red spanish or bermuda onion; a large, sweet tasting, purple-red onion.
shallots also called french shallots, golden shallots or eschalots. Small and elongated, with a brown-skin, they grow in tight clusters similar to garlic.
spring crisp, narrow green-leafed tops and a round sweet white bulb larger than green onions.

PANCETTA an Italian unsmoked bacon; pork belly is cured in salt and spices then rolled into a sausage shape and dried for several weeks.

PAPRIKA ground dried sweet red capsicum (bell pepper); there are many types available, including hot, sweet, mild and smoked.

PINE NUTS also called pignoli; not a nut but a small, cream-coloured kernel from pine cones. They are best roasted before use to bring out the flavour.

POLENTA also called cornmeal; a flour-like cereal of dried corn (maize). Also the dish made from it.

POMEGRANATE a fruit about the size of an orange, with a yellowish shell that turns a rich red colour as it matures. Inside the inedible husk are hundreds of seeds, each wrapped in an edible lucent-crimson pulp having a tangy sweet-sour flavour.

POMELO this large citrus fruit is used commonly in Asian salads and is also very good for making marmalade, due to its high pith content. Remove skin and pith from around the fruit, using a small sharp knife, segment the fruit. If unavailable, use ruby red grapefruit.

POTATO, KIPFLER a small, finger-shaped potato with a nutty flavour; is great baked and in salads.

PRESERVED LEMON whole or quartered salted lemons preserved in a mixture of water, lemon juice or olive oil, and occasionally with spices such as cinnamon, coriander and clove. Use the rind only and rinse well under cold water before using.

QUAIL small, delicate flavoured, domestically grown game birds ranging in weight from 250g to 300g. Also known as partridge.

RADICCHIO Italian in origin; a member of the chicory family. The dark burgundy leaves and strong, bitter flavour can be cooked or eaten raw in salads.

RICE
basmati a white, fragrant long-grained rice; grains fluff up beautifully when cooked. It should be washed several times before cooking.
wild not a true member of the rice family but a very dark brown seed of a North American aquatic grass; has a distinctively nutty flavour and crunchy, resilient texture. Sold on its own or in a blend with basmati or long-grained white rice.

ROCKET (ARUGULA) also rugula and rucola; peppery green leaf eaten raw in salads or used in cooking. Baby rocket leaves are smaller and less peppery.

SAFFRON stigma of a member of the crocus family, available ground or in strands; imparts a yellow-orange colour to food once infused. The quality can vary greatly; the best is the most expensive spice in the world.

SAKE Japan's favourite wine, made from fermented rice, is used for marinating, cooking and in dipping sauces. If sake is unavailable, dry sherry, vermouth or brandy can be substituted. If drinking sake, place in a container then in hot water for 20 minutes to warm through.

SAMBAL OELEK also ulek or olek; an Indonesian salty paste made from ground chillies and vinegar.

SASHIMI fish sold as sashimi has to meet stringent guidelines regarding its handling. We suggest you seek local advice from authorities before eating any raw seafood.

SEAFOOD
lobster (rock lobster) also called cray, spiny lobster, eastern, southern or western lobster. Substitute with balmain or moreton bay bugs.
prawns (shrimp) varieties include, school, king, royal red, Sydney harbour or tiger. Can be bought uncooked (green) or cooked, with or without shells.
scallops a bivalve mollusc with a fluted shell valve; we use scallops that have the coral (roe) attached.

SICHUAN PEPPER
the peppercorns are reddish-brown in colour, with a strong, pungent aroma and a sharp, tingling and mildly spicy taste. Dry-roast to bring out their full flavour; grind with a mortar and pestle.

SOY SAUCE
dark deep brown, almost black in colour; rich, with a thicker consistency than other types. Pungent but not particularly salty; good for marinating.
japanese an all-purpose low-sodium soy sauce with more wheat content than its Chinese counterparts; fermented in barrels and aged. Possibly the best table soy and the one to choose if you only want one variety.
light fairly thin in consistency and, while paler than the others, the saltiest tasting; used in dishes in which the natural colour of the ingredients is to be maintained. Not to be confused with salt-reduced or low-sodium soy sauces.

SPINACH
also called english spinach and incorrectly, silver beet. Baby spinach leaves are best eaten raw in salads; the larger leaves should be added last to soups, stews and stir-fries, and should be cooked until barely wilted.

STAR ANISE
a dried star-shaped pod whose seeds have an astringent aniseed flavour; commonly used to flavour stocks and marinades.

SUGAR
brown a soft, finely granulated sugar retaining molasses for its characteristic colour and flavour.
caster (superfine) finely granulated table sugar.
demerara small-grained golden-coloured crystal sugar.
icing (confectioners') also known as powdered sugar; pulverised granulated sugar crushed together with a small amount of cornflour.
palm also called nam tan pip, jaggery, jawa or gula melaka; made from the sap of the sugar palm tree. Light brown to black in colour and usually sold in rock-hard cakes; substitute with brown sugar.
pure icing (confectioners') also known as powdered sugar.

SUMAC
a purple-red, astringent spice ground from berries growing on shrubs that flourish wild around the Mediterranean; adds a tart, lemony flavour to dips and dressings and goes well with barbecued meat. Can be found in Middle-Eastern food stores.

THYME
a member of the mint family, it has tiny grey-green leaves that give off a pungent minty, light-lemon aroma. Dried thyme comes in both leaf and powder form. Dried thyme should be stored in a cool, dark place for no more than 3 months. Fresh thyme should be stored in the refrigerator, wrapped in a damp paper towel and placed in a sealed bag for no more than a few days.

TOMATOES
canned whole peeled tomatoes in natural juices; available crushed, diced or chopped, sometimes unsalted or reduced salt. Use undrained.
paste triple-concentrated tomato puree.
truss small vine-ripened tomatoes with the vine still attached.

TREACLE
thick, dark syrup not unlike molasses; a by-product of sugar refining.

TURMERIC
also called kamin; a rhizome related to galangal and ginger. Must be grated or pounded to release its acrid aroma and pungent flavour. Known for the golden colour it imparts, fresh turmeric can be substituted with the more commonly found dried powder. Be aware that fresh turmeric stains your hands and plastic utensils (chopping boards, spatulas, the bowl of a food processor).

VANILLA
bean dried, long, thin pod from a tropical golden orchid; the minuscule black seeds inside the bean are used to impart a luscious vanilla flavour in baking and desserts. Place a whole bean in a jar of sugar to make vanilla sugar; a bean can be used three or four times.
extract made by extracting the flavour from the vanilla bean pod; pods are soaked, usually in alcohol, to capture the authentic flavour.
paste made from vanilla pods and contains real seeds. Is highly concentrated – 1 teaspoon replaces a whole vanilla pod. Found in most supermarkets in the baking section.

VIETNAMESE MINT
not a mint at all, but a pungent and peppery narrow-leafed member of the buckwheat family. Not confined to Vietnam, it is also called cambodian mint, pak pai (Thailand), laksa leaf (Indonesia), daun kesom (Singapore) and rau ram in Vietnam.

VINEGAR
balsamic originally from Modena, Italy, there are now many balsamic vinegars on the market. Quality can be determined up to a point by price; use the most expensive sparingly. Aged balsamic is thicker.
cider made from fermented apples.
rice wine is a vinegar used in Asian cooking. Made from rice wine lees (sediment left after fermentation), salt and alcohol.

WASABI
also spelled wasabe; an Asian horseradish used to make the pungent, green-coloured sauce traditionally served with Japanese raw fish dishes; sold in powdered or paste form.

WATERCRESS
a slightly peppery, dark-green leafy vegetable commercially cultivated but also found growing in the wild. Highly perishable, so must be used as soon as possible after purchase.

WITLOF (BELGIAN ENDIVE)
related to and confused with chicory. A versatile vegetable, it tastes as good cooked as it does raw. Grown in darkness like white asparagus to prevent it becoming green.

WOMBOK (NAPA CABBAGE)
also called chinese or peking cabbage; elongated in shape with pale green, crinkly leaves, this is the most common cabbage in South-East Asia. Can be shredded or chopped and eaten raw or braised, steamed or stir-fried.

YOGURT
we use plain full-cream yogurt unless stated otherwise.

ZUCCHINI
also known as courgette.

CONVERSION CHART

MEASURES

One Australian metric measuring cup holds approximately 250ml; one Australian metric tablespoon holds 20ml; one Australian metric teaspoon holds 5ml.

The difference between one country's measuring cups and another's is within a two- or three-teaspoon variance, and will not affect your cooking results. North America, New Zealand and the United Kingdom use a 15ml tablespoon.

All cup and spoon measurements are level. The most accurate way of measuring dry ingredients is to weigh them. When measuring liquids, use a clear glass or plastic jug with the metric markings.

The imperial measurements used in these recipes are approximate only. Measurements for cake pans are approximate only. Using same-shaped cake pans of a similar size should not affect the outcome of your baking. We measure the inside top of the cake pan to determine sizes.

We use large eggs with an average weight of 60g.

DRY MEASURES

METRIC	IMPERIAL
15g	½oz
30g	1oz
60g	2oz
90g	3oz
125g	4oz (¼lb)
155g	5oz
185g	6oz
220g	7oz
250g	8oz (½lb)
280g	9oz
315g	10oz
345g	11oz
375g	12oz (¾lb)
410g	13oz
440g	14oz
470g	15oz
500g	16oz (1lb)
750g	24oz (1½lb)
1kg	32oz (2lb)

LIQUID MEASURES

METRIC	IMPERIAL
30ml	1 fluid oz
60ml	2 fluid oz
100ml	3 fluid oz
125ml	4 fluid oz
150ml	5 fluid oz
190ml	6 fluid oz
250ml	8 fluid oz
300ml	10 fluid oz
500ml	16 fluid oz
600ml	20 fluid oz
1000ml (1 litre)	1¾ pints

LENGTH MEASURES

METRIC	IMPERIAL
3mm	⅛in
6mm	¼in
1cm	½in
2cm	¾in
2.5cm	1in
5cm	2in
6cm	2½in
8cm	3in
10cm	4in
13cm	5in
15cm	6in
18cm	7in
20cm	8in
22cm	9in
25cm	10in
28cm	11in
30cm	12in (1ft)

OVEN TEMPERATURES

The oven temperatures in this book are for conventional ovens; if you have a fan-forced oven, decrease the temperature by 10-20 degrees.

	°C (CELSIUS)	°F (FAHRENHEIT)
Very slow	120	250
Slow	150	300
Moderately slow	160	325
Moderate	180	350
Moderately hot	200	400
Hot	220	425
Very hot	240	475

INDEX

A

allspice 340
almond praline 218
angel gift tag cookies 293
apple
    apple, pear and cranberry juice 108
    apple Pimm's 12
    green grape and apple spritzer 108
    pork rack with sage apples 87
    roasted goose with spiced apples
        and onions 74
    sage apples 87
    turnovers 120
apricots in thyme syrup 224
asparagus
    asparagus salad with spring onion
        and pea vinaigrette 90
    poached eggs with lemon asparagus 117

B

baby chocolate christmas cakes 299
baking paper 340
baking powder 340
banana maple pancakes with pecans 112
basil and pine nut dressing 96
basil dressing 181
bay leaves 340
beans 340
    bean salad with basil dressing 181
    broad bean, pine nut and rocket salad 133
    broad beans and thyme 99
    prosciutto-wrapped prawns
        with bean salad 143
beef
    barbecued fillet of beef with
        caramelised radish and onion 164
    mustard beef canapés 45
    pepper-crusted beef with mustard
        and crème fraîche sauce 174
    roast beef and coleslaw on rye 322
    salt, lemon and rosemary cured beef 16
beetroot 340
    pineapple, carrot and beetroot juice 108
    roasted rosemary and pepper beets 96
bellini 126
berry and yogurt muffins 111

betel leaves 340
bicarbonate of soda 340
biscuits
    angel gift tag cookies 293
    christmas cookies 282
    passionfruit cream 284
    pecorino and nigella seed 11
    spiced wreath biscuits 302
    stained glass christmas cookies 290
blinis
    goat's cheese, with 36
    green onion, with chilli crab salad 20
boozy prunes and ginger 293
bourbon-glazed ham with warm potato
    and celery salad 162
bread 340
    corn 82–3
broad bean, pine nut and rocket salad 133
broad beans and thyme 99
brownie bombs 282
bruschetta, glazed fig 111
brussels sprouts with crispy onions
    and pancetta 90
burghul 340
butter 340
    spiced rum 214
buttermilk 340

C

cakes
    baby chocolate christmas 299
    boiled fruit 269
    celebration christmas 262
    chocolate and sherry cherry 265
    chocolate drambuie fruit 261
    fruit 255
    gluten- and dairy-free spicy fruit 266
    gluten-free fruit and almond loaves 258
    golden glacé fruit 258
    grand marnier fruit 244–5
    hazelnut mud cake with fudge
        frosting 236
    irish pudding 252
    night before fruit 248
    rich chocolate fruit 251
    three-in-one fruit mix 197

campari, orange and soda 15
candied lemon slices 235
candied sweet potato pie 83
capers 340
    herbed salmon with capers and
        fennel remoulade 149
    smoked salmon with 61
capsicum 340
    capsicum and ciabatta crumbs 78
caramel sauce 202
caramelised radish and onion 164
caramels, sea salt and cashew 290
caraway seeds 340
cardamom 340
carrot and turmeric salad 139
carrots, glazed, with hazelnuts 87
celebration christmas cakes 262
champagne cocktail 126
charcuterie plate 139
cheat's frozen christmas pudding 224
cheese 340
    blinis with goat's cheese 36
    cherry, walnut and fetta salad 187
    crostini with fetta, artichokes
        and rocket 23
    double cheese potato gratin 93
    fig, onion and bocconcini tart 58
    ham, egg and cheese toasties 321
    ham, zucchini and fetta loaves 325
    melon, bocconcini and mint salad 133
    onion, thyme and goat's cheese tarts 137
    peach, prosciutto and mozzarella
        salad 190
    pecorino and nigella seed biscuits 11
    ricotta, zucchini and ham wrap 322
    spiced eggplant and haloumi tarts 30
    sweet potato, mint and goat's
        cheese tartlets 42
    tomato, fetta and ham frittatas 328
cheesecake, fruit cake and eggnog 334
cherry and almond stuffing 77
cherry, walnut and fetta salad 187
chervil 341
chicken 341
    caesar salad 314
    chicken and port pâté on polenta
        crisps 19
    chicken caesar on baby cos leaves 48

(*chicken* continued)
    chicken, pork and veal terrine 54
    fried rice 314
    pasta salad 314
    roast balsamic chicken with garlic bread sauce 69
    smoked chicken crostini 39
    wraps 314
chickpea and chilli walnut salad 178
chilli 341
    chickpea and chilli walnut salad 178
    chilli and ginger dressing 48
    chilli crab salad 20
    chilli plum dressing 317
    skewered prawns with chilli marinade 42
chinese cooking wine 341
chocolate 341
    baby chocolate christmas cakes 299
    brownie bombs 282
    choc-orange sauce 214
    choc-orange truffles with boozy prunes and ginger 293
    chocolate and sherry cherry 265
    chocolate drambuie fruit cake 261
    chocolate fig panforte 296
    chocolate orange ice-cream 210–11
    ganache 265
    little chocolate christmas puddings 336
    rich chocolate fruit 251
    yule log 228
chorizo 341
christmas cookies 282
christmas ice-cream pudding bites 339
christmas muffins 283
christmas pudding, frozen 210–11
    cheat's 224
cinnamon 341
    cinnamon sugar 307
classic cosmopolitan cocktail 15
cloves 341
cocoa powder 341
coconut, desiccated 341
cookies *see* biscuits
coriander 341
    roasted vegetables with garlic and coriander oil 102
corn bread 82–3
cornflour 341

cottage loaf, turkey 317
craft
    christmas bauble decoration 311
    christmas stockings 84
    christmas tree, contemporary 9
    christmas tree table setting 34
    christmas wrappings 53
    falling snowflakes 240
    hallway decorations 106, 311
    lollies decorations 273
    table settings 34, 131, 158
    winter wonderland 195
    wreath 158
cranberries 341
    apple, pear and cranberry juice 108
    roast pork with cranberry sauce 65
    turkey, cranberry and peanut salad 325
cream 341
cream of tartar 341
crème fraîche 341
    mustard and crème fraîche sauce 174
    zucchini and corn fritters with 39
crostini 45
    fetta, artichokes and rocket, with 23
    smoked chicken 39
cucumber, pickled 156–7
cumin 341
custard cream 124
custard fruit flans 124
custard powder 341
custard, vanilla bean 214

D

daikon 341
    pickled 33
dressing 178
    basil 181
    basil and pine nut 96
    chilli and ginger 48
    chilli plum 317
    lemon 187
    mustard 99
    mustard and cider 187
    mustard honey 61
    peanut and garlic 184
    salsa verde 140

drinks
    apple, pear and cranberry juice 108
    apple Pimm's 12
    bellini 126
    campari, orange and soda 15
    champagne cocktail 126
    classic cosmopolitan cocktail 15
    eggnog 126
    ginger, orange and pineapple juice 108
    green grape and apple spritzer 108
    lemon, lime and bitters punch 126
    lychee and lime muddle 12
    mulled "wine" cocktail 12
    pineapple, carrot and beetroot juice 108
    pineapple passionfruit spritzer 15
    sparkling raspberry 12
    white chocolate eggnog 15
duck
    barbecued, with caramelised fennel oranges 161
    marinated, with peppered strawberries 134

E

eccles mince pies 123
eggnog 126
    fruit cake and eggnog cheesecake 334
    white chocolate eggnog 15
eggplant 342
    spiced eggplant and haloumi tarts 30
eggs 342
    baked 120
    ham, egg and cheese toasties 321
    masala omelette 117
    poached, with lemon asparagus 117
    quail eggs with dukkah 26
    tomato, fetta and ham frittatas 328

F

fennel 342
    caramelised fennel oranges 161
    fennel, red onion, grapefruit and rocket salad 57
    lobster with fennel salad 153

(fennel continued)
   pork and fennel sausage stuffing 169
   remoulade 149
   warm orange and fennel olives 26
figs
   chocolate fig panforte 296
   fig, almond and mascarpone trifle 218
   fig, onion and bocconcini tart 58
   glazed fig bruschetta 111
   pistachio and fig stuffing 74
fish sauce 342
flans, custard fruit 124
flour 342
forcemeat stuffing 66, 82–3
fresh cherry and pistachio tabbouleh 183
friands, fruit mince 269
fried rice, chicken 314
frittatas, tomato, fetta and ham 328
fritters, zucchini and corn, with crème fraîche 39
frozen christmas pudding 210–11
   cheat's 224
fruit and almond loaves, gluten-free 258
fruit cake and eggnog cheesecake 334
fruit cake cream parfait 328
fruit cake ice-cream terrine 331
fruit cakes *see* cakes
fruit mince 123, 232
fruit mince friands 269
fruit mince pies with spiced hazelnut pastry 287
fruit mince tart with white chocolate cream 232
fruit nut clusters 283
fruit pudding, sticky, with caramel sauce 202
fudge frosting 236

G
ganache 251
   chocolate 265
garlic bread sauce 69
gelatine 342
ginger 342
   ginger marmalade glazed ham 166
   ginger, orange and pineapple juice 108
   steamed fish with ginger and green onion salad 150

gingerbread house 276–7
glacé cherries 342
glacé fruit 342
glazed fruit stollen 304
glucose syrup 342
gluten- and dairy-free spicy fruit cake 266
gluten- and dairy-free steamed pudding 213
gluten-free fruit and almond loaves 258
golden boiled pudding 206–7
golden glacé fruit cake 258
golden syrup 342
goose, roasted, with spiced apples and onions 74
grand marnier fruit cake 244–5
green grape and apple spritzer 108
green olive and currant salsa 153
green onion blinis with chilli crab salad 20
green papaya salad 184

H
ham
   barbecued 146
   bourbon-glazed ham with warm potato and celery salad 162
   ginger marmalade glazed 166
   ham, egg and cheese toasties 321
   ham, zucchini and fetta loaves 325
   ricotta, zucchini and ham wrap 322
   tomato, fetta and ham frittatas 328
harissa 170
hasselback potatoes 93
hazelnuts
   glazed carrots with 87
   hazelnut filling 228
   hazelnut hard sauce 214
   hazelnut mud cake with fudge frosting 236
herb butter 62
herbed salmon with capers and fennel remoulade 149
honey panna cotta with apricots in thyme syrup 224
horseradish 342
hot-smoked trout with young coconut 29

I
ice-cream
   chocolate orange 210–11
   white christmas 221
irish pudding cake 252
italian-style toasted buns 321

J
jewelled macaroons 296

K
kaffir lime leaves 342
kecap manis 342
kitchen string 342
kumara 342

L
lamb
   butterflied, with fresh mint sauce 173
   cutlets with sumac yogurt 45
   rolled lamb shoulder with harissa and couscous stuffing 170
lemon
   dressing 187
   lemon and raspberry semifreddo 235
   lemon and rosemary salt cure 16
   lemon, lime and bitters punch 126
   lemon royal icing 293
   lemon slices, candied 235
   poached eggs with lemon asparagus 117
little chocolate christmas puddings 336
lobster with fennel salad 153
lychees 342
   lychee and lime muddle 12

M
macadamia and pecan shortbread 287
macaroons
   cinnamon and sour cherry 307
   jewelled 296

maple syrup (pure) 342
   banana maple pancakes with pecans 112
marinated duck with peppered
   strawberries 134
marzipan 342
masala omelette 117
mascarpone filling 221
mayonnaise, red wine vinegar 57
melon, bocconcini and mint salad 133
meringue, pistachio 217
mince pies 303
mini christmas puddings 279
mint sauce 173
mirin 342
mixed peel 342
mixed spice 342
morello sour cherries 342
   cinnamon and sour cherry
      macaroons 307
muffins
   berry and yogurt 111
   christmas 283
mulled "wine" cocktail 12
mushrooms 342–3
   pickled 139
mustard 343
   dressing 99
   mustard and cider dressing 187
   mustard and crème fraîche sauce 174
   mustard beef canapés 45

N

new york-style deli sandwich 322
nigella seeds 343
   pecorino and nigella seed biscuits 11
night before fruit cake 248
nori 343
nutmeg 343

O

oil 343
olives
   warm orange and fennel 26
onion 343
   asparagus salad with spring onion
      and pea vinaigrette 90

(*onion* continued)
   brussels sprouts with crispy onions
      and pancetta 90
   fennel, red onion, grapefruit and
      rocket salad 57
   fig, onion and bocconcini tart 58
   onion, thyme and goat's cheese tarts 137
   roasted goose with spiced apples
      and onions 74
   steamed fish with ginger and
      green onion salad 150
orange and fennel olives, warm 26
orange pudding with rum sauce 227
oranges, caramelised fennel 161
oysters with chilli and ginger dressing 48

P

pancetta 343
   brussels sprouts with crispy onions
      and pancetta 90
panettone toast with peaches and
   blueberries 312
panettone with mascarpone and
   raspberries 221
panforte, chocolate fig 296
paprika 343
parsnips, roasted caramelised 102
passionfruit cream 284
pâté, chicken and port, on polenta
   crisps 19
pea, mint and almond salad 187
peach, prosciutto and mozzarella
   salad 190
peanut and garlic dressing 184
peanut caramel 156–7
peanut nam jim 29
pear and witlof salad 99
pecorino and nigella seed biscuits 11
peppered strawberries 134
pickled cucumber 156–7
pickled daikon 33
pickled mushrooms 139
pies
   eccles mince 123
   fruit mince, with spiced hazelnut
      pastry 287

pine nuts 343
   basil and pine nut dressing 96
   broad bean, pine nut and
      rocket salad 133
   tomato, basil and pine nut salad 96
pineapple passionfruit spritzer 15
pistachio and fig stuffing 74
pistachio meringue with white
   peaches and berries 217
polenta 343
   crisps 19
pomegranate 343
   quail salad with pomegranate
      dressing 146
pomelo 343
pork
   chicken, pork and veal terrine 54
   pork and fennel sausage stuffing 169
   pork hock with peanut caramel
      and pickled cucumber 156–7
   pork loin with spiced orange relish 177
   pork rack with sage apples 87
   roast leg of pork with pears
      and parsnips 73
   roast pork loin with rosemary gravy 78
   roast, with cranberry sauce 65
   salad with chilli plum dressing 317
porridge with banana and brazil nuts 112
potato
   double cheese potato gratin 93
   hasselback 93
   kipfler 343
   pancakes with smoked salmon
      and dill cream 114
   warm kipfler and cucumber salad
      with dill 190
   warm potato and celery salad 162
prawns
   prawn cocktail with zucchini and
      mint salad 143
   prosciutto-wrapped prawns with
      bean salad 143
   skewered, with chilli marinade 42
preserved lemon 343
prosciutto and pear stuffing 62
prosciutto-wrapped prawns with
   bean salad 143
prunes and ginger, boozy 293

puddings
  boiled 200–1
  cheat's frozen christmas 224
  frozen christmas 210–11
  gluten- and dairy-free steamed 213
  golden boiled 206–7
  little chocolate christmas 336
  mini christmas 279
  orange, with rum sauce 227
  steamed 200–1
  sticky fruit pudding with caramel sauce 202
  three-in-one fruit mix 197

Q

quail 343
  eggs with dukkah 26
  salad with pomegranate dressing 146
  quail salad with pomegranate dressing 146

R

radicchio 343
radish and onion, caramelised 164
red wine vinegar dressing 183
red wine vinegar mayonnaise 57
relish, spiced orange 177
remoulade, fennel 149
rice 343
rich chocolate fruit cake 251
ricotta, zucchini and ham wrap 322
roasts
  pork rack with sage apples 87
  roast balsamic chicken with garlic bread sauce 69
  roast leg of pork with pears and parsnips 73
  roast pork loin with rosemary gravy 78
  roast pork with cranberry sauce 65
  roast turkey with corn bread and candied sweet potato pie 82–3
  roast turkey with prosciutto and pear stuffing 62
  roasted caramelised parsnips 102
  roasted goose with spiced apples and onions 74
  roasted rosemary and pepper beets 96

(*roasts* continued)
  roasted vegetables 65
  roasted vegetables with garlic and coriander oil 102
  slow-roasted turkey with wild rice seasoning 70
  traditional turkey with forcemeat stuffing 66
  turkey roll with cherry and almond stuffing 77
rocket 343
  broad bean, pine nut and rocket salad 133
  crostini with fetta, artichokes and rocket 23
  fennel, red onion, grapefruit and rocket salad 57
rum sauce 227

S

saffron 343
  scallops with saffron cream 23
sake 343
  wasabi and sake cured kingfish 33
salad
  asparagus salad with spring onion and pea vinaigrette 90
  bean salad with basil dressing 181
  broad bean, pine nut and rocket 133
  carrot and turmeric 139
  cherry, walnut and fetta 187
  chicken caesar 314
  chicken caesar on baby cos leaves 48
  chicken pasta 314
  chickpea and chilli walnut 178
  chilli crab 20
  fennel, red onion, grapefruit and rocket 57
  fresh cherry and pistachio tabbouleh 183
  green papaya 184
  lobster with fennel 153
  melon, bocconcini and mint 133
  pea, mint and almond 187
  peach, prosciutto and mozzarella 190
  pear and witlof 99
  pork salad with chilli plum dressing 317
  prawn cocktail with zucchini and mint 143

(*salad* continued)
  prosciutto-wrapped prawns with bean 143
  quail salad with pomegranate dressing 146
  steamed fish with ginger and green onion 150
  strawberry and smoked salmon 133
  tomato, basil and pasta 133
  tomato, basil and pine nut 96
  turkey, cranberry and peanut 325
  warm kipfler and cucumber salad with dill 190
  warm potato and celery 162
salmon ceviche 36
salsa, green olive and currant 153
salsa verde dressing 140
salt, lemon and rosemary cured beef 16
sambal oelek 343
sashimi 343
sauce
  caramel 202
  choc-orange 214
  garlic bread 69
  hazelnut hard 214
  mint 173
  mustard and crème fraîche 174
  rum 227
scallops with saffron cream 23
sea salt and cashew caramels 290
seafood 344
  chilli crab salad 20
  herbed salmon with capers and fennel remoulade 149
  hot-smoked trout with young coconut 29
  lobster with fennel salad 153
  oysters with chilli and ginger dressing 48
  potato pancakes with smoked salmon and dill cream 114
  prawn cocktail with zucchini and mint salad 143
  prosciutto-wrapped prawns with bean salad 143
  salmon ceviche 36
  scallops with saffron cream 23
  skewered prawns with chilli marinade 42
  smoked salmon with capers 61
  steamed fish with ginger and green onion salad 150

(*seafood* continued)
    strawberry and smoked salmon salad 133
    wasabi and sake cured kingfish 33
semifreddo, lemon and raspberry 235
shortbread, macadamia and pecan 287
sichuan pepper 344
skewered prawns with chilli marinade 42
slice, white christmas 255
smoked chicken crostini 39
smoked salmon with capers 61
smoked trout salad with salsa verde dressing 140
sour cherry curd 307
soy sauce 344
sparkling raspberry 12
spiced eggplant and haloumi tarts 30
spiced orange relish 177
spiced rum butter 214
spiced wreath biscuits 302
spinach 344
stained glass christmas cookies 290
star anise 344
steamed fish with ginger and green onion salad 150
sticky fruit pudding with caramel sauce 202
stollen, glazed fruit 304
strawberry and smoked salmon salad 133
stuffing
    cherry and almond 77
    forcemeat 66
    pistachio and fig 74
    pork and fennel sausage 169
    prosciutto and pear 62
sugar 344
    cinnamon 307
sumac 344
    yogurt 45
sweet potato, mint and goat's cheese tartlets 42

T

tabbouleh, fresh cherry and pistachio 182
tartlets, sweet potato, mint and goat's cheese 42

tarts
    fig, onion and bocconcini 58
    fruit mince, with white chocolate cream 232
    onion, thyme and goat's cheese 137
    spiced eggplant and haloumi 30
terrine
    chicken, pork and veal 54
    fruit cake ice-cream 331
three-in-one fruit mix 197
    boiled or steamed pudding 200–1
    fruit cake 255
    mince pies 303
thyme 344
    apricots in thyme syrup 224
    broad beans and 99
    onion, thyme and goat's cheese tarts 137
tiramisu torte 231
tomatoes 344
    tomato, basil and pasta salad 133
    tomato, basil and pine nut salad 96
    tomato, fetta and ham frittatas 328
torte, tiramisu 231
treacle 344
trifle, fig, almond and mascarpone 218
truffles, choc-orange, with boozy prunes and ginger 293
tuile leaves 228
turkey
    cottage loaf 317
    italian-style turkey roll with pork and fennel sausage stuffing 169
    roast with corn bread and candied sweet potato pie 82–3
    roast turkey with prosciutto and pear stuffing 62
    roll with cherry and almond stuffing 77
    slow-roasted, with wild rice seasoning 70
    toasted turkish, on 321
    traditional with forcemeat stuffing 66
    turkey and salad pocket 322
    turkey and tomato salsa quesadillas 321
    turkey, cranberry and peanut salad 325
turmeric 344
    carrot and turmeric salad 139
turnovers, apple 120

V

vanilla 344
    vanilla bean custard 214
veal
    chicken, pork and veal terrine 54
vegetables, roasted 65
vegetables, roasted, with garlic and coriander oil 102
vietnamese mint 344
vinegar 344

W

wasabi 344
    wasabi and sake cure 33
watercress 344
white chocolate
    cream 232
    eggnog 15
    white christmas slice 255
wild rice seasoning 70
witlof 344
    pear and witlof salad 99
wombok 344
wraps
    chicken 314
    ricotta, zucchini and ham 322

Y

yogurt 344
    sumac 45
yule log 228

Z

zabaglione cream 218
zucchini 344
    ham, zucchini and fetta loaves 325
    prawn cocktail with zucchini and mint salad 143
    ricotta, zucchini and ham wrap 322
    zucchini and corn fritters with crème fraîche 39

First published in 2011 by ACP Books, Sydney
This edition published in 2011, reprinted in 2012
ACP Books are published by ACP Magazines Limited
a division of Nine Entertainment Co.

ACP BOOKS
Publishing Director, ACP Magazines Gerry Reynolds
Publisher Sally Wright
Editor-in-chief Susan Tomnay
Creative director & designer Hieu Chi Nguyen
Senior editor Stephanie Kistner
Food director Pamela Clark
Senior food editor Rebecca Squadrito
Sales & rights director Brian Cearnes
Acting marketing manager Sonia Scali
Senior business analyst Rebecca Varela
Operations manager David Scotto
Production controller Corinne Whitsun-Jones

Published by ACP Books, a division of ACP Magazines Ltd,
54 Park St, Sydney; GPO Box 4088, Sydney, NSW 2001.
phone (02) 9282 8618; fax (02) 9126 3702
acpbooks@acpmagazines.com.au; www.acpbooks.com.au

Printed with C&C Offset Printing, China.

Australia Distributed by Network Services Company,
phone 1300 131 169; fax 1300 360 165
networkcontactus@networkservicescompany.com.au
New Zealand Distributed by Southern Publishers Group,
phone +64 9 4192635; fax +64 9 4192634
hub@spg.co.nz
South Africa Distributed by PSD Promotions,
phone +27 11 392 6065/6/7; fax +27 11 392 6079/80
www.psdpromotions.com

A catalogue in publication record for this book is available
from the National Library of Australia.
ISBN: 978-1-74245-211-1

© ACP Magazines Ltd 2011
ABN 18 053 273 546
This publication is copyright. No part of it may be reproduced or transmitted
in any form without the written permission of the publishers.

Photographer Ian Wallace
Food & craft stylist Louise Pickford
Additional food styling Jennifer Tolhurst
Food preparation Sharon Kennedy, Elizabeth Macri
Cover Lemon and raspberry semifreddo, page 235.

The publisher would like to thank the following for props used in photography:
Emerald and Ella www.emeraldandella.com.au; Newspaper Taxi
www.newspapertaxi.com.au; Paper 2 www.paper2.com.au; Papier D'Amour
www.papierdamour.com.au; Seasonal Concepts www.seasonalconcepts.com.au;
Alfresco Emporium www.alfrescoemporium.com.au; Camargue (02) 9960 6234;
Exhibit Lighting www.exhibit.net.au; Flora & Ceres www.floraandceres.com.au;
French Heritage www.frenchheritagefurniture.com.au; Ici et La www.icietla.com.au;
Imagine This www.imagine-this.com.au; Jasper Conran www.jasperconran.com;
Kate Spade www.katespadechina.com.au; Liley & Liley (02) 9958 3575;
Redelman Fabrics & Wallcoverings www.redelman.com; Royal Doulton
www.royalalbertchina.com.au; The Christmas Warehouse
www.christmaswarehouse.com.au; Villeroy and Boch Australia
1800 252 770 shop.villeroy-boch.com/au_en;
Vixen & Velvet www.vixenandvelvet.com;
Waterford Wedgewood www.wedgwood.com.au

To order books, phone 136 116 (within Australia) or
order online at www.acpbooks.com.au
Send recipe enquiries to:
recipeenquiries@acpmagazines.com.au